Imperial Relations in the Age of Laurier

Canadian Historical Readings

A selection of articles from the *Canadian Historical Review*
and other volumes

1 *Approaches to Canadian History*
2 *Upper Canadian Politics in the 1850's*
3 *Confederation*
4 *Politics of Discontent*
5 *Constitutionalism and Nationalism in Lower Canada*
6 *Imperial Relations in the Age of Laurier*
7 *Minorities, Schools, and Politics*
8 *Conscription 1917*

Edited by Ramsay Cook / Craig Brown / Carl Berger

Imperial Relations in the Age of Laurier

Essays by
H. Blair Neatby/Craig Brown/H. Pearson Gundy
James A. Colvin
Norman Penlington/James Eayrs

Introduction by Carl Berger

University of Toronto Press

Contents

Introduction

CARL BERGER

IMPERIALISM IS A LOADED WORD. It long ago ceased to be an instrument of analysis and became a slogan that conjured up images of economic exploitation and spheres of influence, the domination of the weak by the ruthless and the strong, and incessant conflict and war. In the context of Canadian history its meaning is rather more prosaic and ambiguous. Though it marched under various banners, imperialism, or "imperial federation," or "imperial unity" simply aimed at the strengthening of the British Empire through economic, military, and naval co-operation and through constitutional changes which would give Canada some influence in the formulation of imperial foreign policy.

While English-speaking Canadians had always celebrated their pride of place within the Empire and were appreciative of the advantages that such membership conferred, organized movements for cementing the British connection appeared only in the later 1880's. Branches of the Imperial Federation League, which had been founded in London in 1884, were set up in the dominion and the idea of imperial unity was sent into battle against the Liberal party's commercial policy of unrestricted reciprocity with the United States. Much of the appeal of imperialism during these years was rooted in a sense of insecurity and fear produced by the failure of the National Policy to generate economic integration, by the spectre of continentalism, and by the cultural conflict triggered by the execution of Louis Riel. As an antidote to unrestricted reciprocity the Imperial Federation League in Canada advanced the policy of an imperial preferential tariff system. Though such a proposal was ultimately doomed to failure because the British commitment to free trade was unshakeable, and though the sense of pessimism concerning the national future evaporated after the mid-1890's, the imperial movement, in both Canada and Britain, reached its high tide during the early years of the Laurier period. In 1895 Joseph Chamberlain was appointed colonial secretary; in 1898 Lord Minto took up the office of governor general and Major-General Hutton was named general officer commanding. These three, together with their Canadian sympathizers, were untiring in their efforts to secure Canadian support for the Empire in the Boer War. Imperial defence was central to imperial relations in the age of Laurier, not only because it raised the question of Canada's relation to the outside world and the issue of how the responsibilities of nationhood were to be assumed, but also because a contribution to the defence of the Empire was regarded as a device by which the dominion could obtain some power over external affairs. Laurier had earlier expressed enthusiasm for the imperial ideal and the preferential tariff of 1897 was widely hailed as a step toward its realization; but from the consequences of the Boer War, and especially the alienation of French Canada, he quickly recoiled. His position at the Colonial Conferences amounted to what John Dafoe, editor of the *Winnipeg Free Press*, called "fifteen years of saying 'no'" to all centralizing schemes.

In the traditional liberal nationalist historiography the movement for imperial unity was set within a broad interpretative framework of the Canadian past. This interpretation, perhaps best expressed in O. D. Skelton's *Life and Letters of Sir Wilfrid Laurier* (Toronto, 1921) and Dafoe's *Laurier, A Study in Canadian Politics* (Toronto, 1922), was itself a by-product of the struggle for dominion autonomy. Its central theme and organizing principle was that Canadian history was essentially the story of a steady and progressive rise from a colonial position to that of free and autonomous nationhood. The steps which marked this great ascent were chiefly those involving the acquisition of responsible government and the extensions of the principle of self-government into the spheres of commercial and foreign policy. Seen from within this perspective, imperialism threatened to divert the flow of history from its proper and predetermined channel. "It took many forms, wore many disguises," wrote one of its sternest critics, "but in its secret purposes it was unchangeable and unwearying." It sought some kind of central council in which imperial foreign policy would be defined and it would, if successful, not only subvert the freedom of action which Canada had already attained, but it would also perpetually subordinate the interests of Canada to those of Britain. Such anti-imperialists as Dafoe and Skelton, the French-Canadian nationalist Henri Bourassa, and the liberal intellectual Goldwin Smith opposed the movement for varied reasons but all concurred that it was sponsored by certain circles in order to consolidate the military resources of the Empire for the power, prestige, and profit of England. The attempt to secure a voice on imperial matters in exchange for tribute for defence struck Bourassa as gross and vulgar bargaining. Imperialism, he said, was ". . . LA CONTRIBUTION DES COLONIES AUX GUERRES DE L'ANGLETERRE, en hommes et en deniers, en hommes surtout." According to its critics, imperialism was reactionary in purpose, militarist in spirit, and ignoble in motive. The phrase Canadian imperialism was a contradiction in terms: those Canadians who supported imperial unity were hopelessly confused and colonially minded.

This, in substance, was the indictment and characterization of imperialism which passed into the history books and, to an extent, still prevails in certain quarters. It has, for instance, been restated with much feeling in Joseph Schull's *Laurier, The First Canadian* (Toronto, 1965). The passage of time, however, gives us a different point of vantage and suggests different questions. A large step toward a reinterpretation of this subject was made by Norman Penlington's *Canada and Imperialism, 1896–1899* (Toronto, 1965) which not only destroyed the myth that Canadian participation in the Boer War was primarily the result of Downing Street interference and the manipulation of news, but demonstrated as well how powerful were the pressures for involvement arising from within English-speaking Canada. It has also been suggested that nothing so cataclysmic as a conflict between "Canadian nationalism" and a subservient colonialism ever took place, and that in fact many Canadian imperialists were nationalists who believed that national status could be better secured within the framework of the Empire than outside of it. They believed that Canadian and British interests on fundamental matters were not necessarily irreconcilable and that a genuine alliance of equal nations was in accord with both tradition and the realities of power on the North American continent. Carrying the process of revision one step further, D. G. Creighton has proposed a radically different approach to Laurier's concept of nationalism:

Laurier, we are told, foiled the conspiracy of the British imperialists, though it could be argued that this conspiracy was nothing more sinister than an attempt to fit the British empire, as it then was, for the terrible times which in fact overtook it in the second decade of the century. Laurier was largely responsible for the defeat of these attempts. But for what purpose? What part did he want Canada to play in the empire, or in the world as a whole? He is admiringly called a nationalist; yet he seems to have feared the maturity and to have avoided the responsibilities of nationalism. He told Dundonald, the General Officer Commanding the Canadian Militia, that he need not take the militia seriously, since Canada was protected by the Monroe Doctrine. It was eight years before he tried to make good his promise to provide for Canada's own naval defence. On the morrow of the Alaskan boundary settlement, he had clearly implied that Canada should take the conduct of her foreign policy into her own hands. Yet it was not until 1909 that he established the Department of External Affairs, and even then the portfolio was given to an unimportant hack politician from Ottawa, Charles Murphy. If this is Canadian nationalism, it is an extremely negative kind, a nationalism which, in its casual acceptance of imperial forms and benefits and its determined rejection of imperial duties, is not very far away from the dependent colonialism of Bourassa.

The articles reprinted in this collection do not of course pretend to present all facets of the movement for imperial unity, nor do they offer final answers to all the questions it raises. What they do provide, however, are detailed studies of certain crucial episodes in imperial relations, notably the tensions between Laurier and Hutton and Minto; a re-examination of the background to the preferential tariff of 1897; penetrating glimpses into the thought of Laurier and Goldwin Smith; and an assessment of the Round Table groups in Canada. If a reading of these articles deepens the appreciation for the complexities of the problem the purpose of reprinting them will have been served.

Those who wish to pursue the subject further might best begin with the books by Skelton and Dafoe, both of which are available in the Carleton Library paperback series. R. M. Dawson, *The Development of Dominion Status, 1900–1936* (Oxford, 1937) and Mason Wade, *The French Canadians, 1760–1945* (Toronto, 1955) follow a similar approach, as do Elisabeth Wallace, *Goldwin Smith, Victorian Liberal* (Toronto, 1957) and R. Rumilly, *Henri Bourassa* (Montreal, 1953). D. G. Creighton, "The Victorians and the Empire," *Canadian Historical Review*, XIX (June, 1938) and J. E. Tyler, *The Struggle for Imperial Unity, 1868–95* (London, 1938) are helpful background studies. There are two superb essays on the context in which the debate over imperialism took place – one on the 1890's by J. T. Saywell, the other on the new century by H. Blair Neatby – in J. M. S. Careless and R. C. Brown, eds., *The Canadians, 1867–1967* (Toronto, 1967). André Siegfried, *The Race Question in Canada* (Carleton Library, Toronto, 1966), originally published in 1906, offers a perceptive commentary on the Canadian political scene in general and imperialism in particular.

Two studies of the campaign for imperial preference are B. H. Brown, *The Tariff Reform Movement in Great Britain, 1881–1895* (New York, 1943) and chapter five of R. C. Brown, *Canada's National Policy 1883–1900: A Study in Canadian-American Relations* (Princeton, 1964). Exhaustive treatments of the question of imperial defence are D. C. Gordon, *The Dominion Partnership in Imperial Defense, 1870–1914* (Baltimore, 1965) and R. A. Preston, *Canada and "Imperial Defense": A Study of the Origins of the British Commonwealth's Defense Organization, 1867–1919* (Toronto, 1967). On the debate over naval defence see G. N. Tucker, *The Naval Service of Canada* (Ottawa, 1952), volume I, and Henry Borden, ed., *Sir Robert Laird Borden: His Memoirs* (Toronto, 1938). A sympathetic treatment of Minto is given in John Buchan, *Lord Minto: A Memoir* (London, 1924), and the Governor General's own reflections are in F. H. Underhill, ed., "Lord Minto on His Governor Generalship," *Canadian Historical Review*, XL (June, 1959). A study of British attitudes to Empire is A. P. Thornton, *The Imperial Idea and Its Enemies* (London, 1959): the Chamberlain position has been described in volume three of *The Life of Joseph Chamberlain* (London, 1934) by J. L. Garvin and volume four (London, 1951) by J. Amery. Carroll Quigley, "The Round Table Groups in Canada, 1908–1938," *Canadian Historical Review*, XLIII (September, 1962), draws upon British material and is a useful supplement to the article by James Eayrs.

Apart from Penlington's *Canada and Imperialism* little has been written about the motives and ideas of the Canadian imperialists, though J. S. Willison, *Sir George Parkin* (London, 1929) and G. T. Denison, *The Struggle for Imperial Unity* (Toronto, 1909) do offer revealing glimpses of two figures who were most active in Canada in the later 1880's and early 1890's. F. H. Underhill, *The Image of Confederation* (Toronto, 1964) contains some brilliant insights into their political outlook.

Laurier and Imperialism

H. BLAIR NEATBY

A DISCUSSION of any aspect of Sir Wilfrid Laurier's career must begin with the recognition that Laurier believed that the relationship between the English-Canadian and the French-Canadian societies was the central problem in Canadian politics. As he wrote to a friend in 1904: "My object is to consolidate Confederation, and to bring our people long estranged from each other, gradually to become a nation. This is the supreme issue. Everything else is subordinate to that idea." [1] It was inevitable that Laurier should focus his attention on the problem of racial harmony within Confederation. As a member of the minority group, and as a leader of a political party which depended upon political support from both racial groups, he was constantly conscious of the need to devise a political policy acceptable to both groups. Even before Laurier became Prime Minister, the Riel crisis and the Manitoba Schools Question had sharply divided Canadians. Thus, when in office, Laurier instinctively considered political problems in terms of avoiding friction between English- and French-Canadians. One such political problem, of direct concern to us, was the question of Canada's relation to the Empire. English-Canadians and French-Canadians differed in their attitude to the Empire, and Laurier had to bear in mind these different attitudes.

To English-Canadians, imperialism was an attitude or a sentiment. Imperialism in Canada had no connection with Marxist imperialism, the 'last stage of monopoly capitalism'. Monopoly capitalism was not unknown in Canada, but for it Canadians had invented the phrase 'National Policy'. Nor was Canadian imperialism closely associated with the mission of 'bearing the white man's burden'. Canadians were too concerned with establishing themselves in North America to become involved in carrying their civilization to others. In Canada, imperialism had a meaning of its own. Broadly speaking, it meant the consciousness of belonging to the British Empire; in practice it meant a devotion to England, the heart of the Empire.

This affection for England took various forms. The most articulate form of Canadian imperialism was based on the assumption of racial superiority; the belief that Anglo-Saxons were destined for world leadership. This vision of a militant Anglo-Saxondom appealed to some English-Canadians, to whom a united Anglo-Saxon Empire seemed preferable to the relative obscurity of an isolated colony. Thus in 1892   George Parkin published a book entitled *Imperial Federation*, significantly subtitled 'The Problem of National Unity'. [2] Parkin argued that there was already an imperial unity based on the common racial origins of British subjects at home and in the colonies. It was natural for men like Parkin to look forward to a political union

[1] Public Archives of Canada, Laurier Papers, 92017, W.L. to W. Gregory, 11 Nov., 1904.
[2]   George Parkin, *Imperial Federation*, (London, 1892).

Reprinted from Canadian Historical Association, *Report*, 1955

which would reflect this racial unity. Such extreme Canadian imperialists merit attention because they were a vocal group, and to many French-Canadians at least, seemed representative of all Canadian imperialists.

Racial imperialism was not typical of English-Canadians. More common was the imperialism of those bound to the old country by less clearly formulated sentiments. Many Canadians were British emigrants, or sons of British emigrants, who felt a natural affection for their Motherland. Others were nurtured on the traditions of the United Empire Loyalists and so developed a loyalty to Great Britain which was often firmly founded on family or social pride. Added to this was the appeal of patriotic English literature, and especially English poetry, at a time when such literature had no domestic Canadian rival. However intangible and undefined such sentiments may have been, they were ever-present factors to be reckoned with in Canadian politics, as both Macdonald and Laurier knew.

But there was yet another form of Canadian imperialism; another way in which Canadians were conscious of belonging to the Empire and of being indebted to England. And this form is especially relevant because Sir Wilfrid Laurier was such an imperialist. This was the imperialism based on a respect for the principles, and especially the political principles, which Great Britain seemed to represent. To such imperialists, pride in the Empire was based on the belief that the British Empire was the bulwark of liberty and justice in the world. This might be described as intellectual imperialism rather than racial or emotional imperialism. Being a reasoned rather than an emotional attachment to England, it was the most moderate form of imperialism, but it was nonetheless significant.

In French-Canadians, Canadian imperialism evoked much different responses. Appeals to the unity of the Anglo-Saxon race could arouse nothing but repulsion. Indeed, the counterpart of the racial imperialists among French-Canadians was that group of extreme *nationalistes* who looked forward to the creation of a French-Canadian nation in North America. [3] Similarly, the sentimental attachment felt by English-Canadians for the Mother Country was duplicated among French-Canadians by a love for the land of their birth. And the political attitude of French-Canadians was to a large extent determined by their desire for survival as a racial, linguistic and cultural group. Any form of political unity for the Empire would so reduce their influence as to endanger this survival. Many French-Canadians respected and appreciated an Empire in which Canada had been granted self-government, and in which the minority in Canada were given certain guarantees of language, religion and law. Yet even here, their concern was with the preservation of what they considered to be their rights. In view of the Riel episode and the Manitoba Schools Question, it seemed unlikely that their rights would be extended. Thus French-Canadians in general were suspicious of any form of imperialism. Any changes in Canada stemming from devotion to England were not likely to improve their chances of survival.

[3] See *Québec, La Verité,* 1 June, 1905, for statement by J. P. Tardivel.

Sir Wilfrid Laurier had stronger imperialist sentiments than many of his compatriots. Naturally, he too lacked the strong emotional attachment to Great Britain based on the concept of Anglo-Saxon superiority as well as the sentimental attachment to Great Britain as the Motherland. But Laurier did have a sincere respect for the British political system, and for British political ideals, and even for British society. This respect for Britain is apparent at the outset of Laurier's career. His attitude as a young politician may be illustrated by his famous speech on political liberalism in 1877.

This speech was delivered at a time when the Liberal Party in Quebec was threatened with extinction. The Roman Catholic clergy had virtually identified the Party with the Catholic-liberal movement in Europe, the movement within the Roman Catholic church by which some men had hoped to reach a compromise between the church and the liberal democratic ideas of the mid-nineteenth century, but which had been condemned by the Syllabus of Errors in 1864. And the episcopacy of the Province had openly declared its intention to intervene in politics whenever the sin of Catholic-liberalism was apparent. [4]

Laurier's speech was a reply to the charge of Catholic-liberalism. He of course found it necessary to deny that the Liberal Party still adhered to the anti-clerical policy of social revolution advocated by the *Rouges* in the past. But of more significance was his attempt to distinguish between Catholic-liberalism and political liberalism. His argument was surprising, in view of the continental origin of the problem and the background of the man himself. It must be remembered that the radicalism of the *Rouges* had been transplanted to Quebec from France, that the extreme clericalism in Quebec had its counterpart in France, and that such compromises as the separation of church and state had their advocates in France. And discussing this problem was Laurier, a young French-Canadian lawyer, educated at L'Assomption College, articled to a French-Canadian law firm in Montreal, practising law in a small French-Canadian town, entering politics at an early age; all this was typical of an ambitious French-Canadian of the period. And yet Laurier did not turn to the history of French Canada to defend his political philosophy, he did not claim to be following in the footsteps of Lafontaine or Cartier. Nor did this French-Canadian turn to French sources to support his arguments; he included no quotations from Montalembert or Lacordaire in spite of the fact that these men had written on the similar problem in France. Instead, this French-Canadian included in his speech two lengthy quotations from Macaulay and supplemented them with three verses from Tennyson. [5] Macaulay and Tennyson are not cosmopolitan literary figures; among historians and poets they seem peculiarly English in their beliefs and prejudices. It is significant that Laurier should turn to them when analyzing the political philosophy of the Liberal Party in Quebec. Even at the beginning of his career he instinctively turned to Great Britain as the source of his political ideas.

4 *Mandements, lettres pastorales, circulaires et autres documents publiés dans le diocèse de Montréal*, (Montreal, 1887), VII, 211.

5 U. Barthe, ed., *Wilfrid Laurier on the Platform*, 1871-1890, (Quebec, 1890), pp. 51-80.

In this speech Laurier made it clear that to him, English liberalism represented the principles of liberty and political justice. "Liberty as it has been practised in France has nothing very attractive about it. The French have had the name of liberty, but they have not yet had liberty itself." [6]   Laurier attributed political liberty in Canada "to the liberal institutions by which we are governed, institutions which we owe to our forefathers and the wisdom of the mothercountry." [7] In this speech he refers to the achievements of Fox, O'Connell, Grey and Russell to illustrate this political liberty and justice. Twenty years later, on the death of Gladstone, he selected as Gladstone's supreme quality, "his intense humanity, his paramount sense of right, his abhorrence of injustice, wrong and oppression wherever to be found . . . ." [8]   Always, Laurier found in English politicians the political principles to which he himself subscribed.

Laurier found much to admire in nineteenth century English liberalism because he too was a nineteenth century liberal in his views on economics, society and politics. A firm believer in the right of private property, he could even express regret that Canada had no constitutional counterpart of the American 'due process of the law' clause. "I have often thought it would be well to introduce such an amendment to our own constitution. The provisions of the American constitution protecting the sacredness of contract have been a source of incalculable strength to the union." [9]   Laurier even considered that he was a free-trader. The exigencies of Canadian politics or, less cynically, the necessity for a diversified Canadian economy, explained the Liberal tariff policy after 1896, but this did not represent a change in Laurier's economic philosophy. Even in 1909 he could describe himself as "a free-trader sound in theory, but somewhat deficient in practice." [10]

It is worth noting that this emphasis on individual rights did not mean that Laurier was an ardent democrat in the equalitarian sense. Again he found much to attract him even in the social structure of English politics. In 1877 he extolled the peers of England who had sacrificed their privileges for the benefit of their fellow beings. [11]   In 1909, during the Parliament Bill controversy, Laurier wrote in almost nostalgic vein about the decline of the English aristocracy. "I am sorry that the aristocracy did not rise to the occasion. The old order of things must give way. It made England very great, but has served its time and must be replaced by the new force which is coming to the front everywhere: democracy." [12]   These are the sentiments of a man who himself had the charm, the dignity and the reserve of a *grand seigneur*. Thus Laurier's respect for British political traditions went beyond intellectual appreciation, and even involved a sentimental admiration for the political role of the old Whig aristocracy.

[6] *Ibid.*, p. 73.
[7] *Ibid.*, p. 78.
[8] Canada, House of Commons, *Debates*, 26 May, 1898, p. 6118.
[9] Laurier Papers, 161567, W.L. to W. Nesbitt, 3 Nov. 1909.
[10] Laurier Papers, 159367, photostat of inscription in book, 1 Sep., 1909.
[11] Barthe, ed., *Laurier on the Platform*, p. 65.
[12] Laurier Papers, 164110, W.L. to J. Sutherland, 25 Dec., 1909.

But of greater significance to Laurier was the political aspect of the English liberal philosophy. Laurier's predilections were political rather than economic. And the liberal emphasis on individual rights in the political sphere had a natural appeal to a French-Canadian Liberal. The answer to clerical interference in the 1870's was to be found in the individual liberty of the elector. In 1886, Laurier could defend the Métis of western Canada on political grounds, and so avoid appeals based on race or religion. The French-Canadian emphasis on provincial rights and, later, on minority rights was also a natural development of this liberalism. The French-Canadian minority in Canada was dependent upon the tolerance and the sense of justice of the English-Canadian majority, and these were the very qualities emphasized by liberal philosophy. Nor is it irrelevant that in the early years of his political life, Laurier found himself closely associated with Edward Blake. In spite of the differences in religious and social background and even in temperament, Blake and Laurier were liberals of the same mould. And Blake, more than any other English-Canadian of the period, seemed able to apply these English liberal standards of tolerance and political justice to French-Canadians at a time when racial intolerance was so prevalent. This friendship must have confirmed Laurier's belief that English political principles could provide a solution for the problem of racial harmony in Canada. It was this respect for British political traditions which helps to explain Laurier's attitude to imperial problems in later years.

Laurier's liberal philosophy could not make him an Imperial Federationist. Imperial federation — or any other scheme of imperial centralization — was out of the question for a French-Canadian or for any politician interested in racial harmony in Canada. But also, the principle of individual liberty in imperial relations meant local autonomy. Laurier believed that it was the recognition of the political rights of the separate colonies which had made the survival of the Empire possible. Thus he regarded imperial federation as the negation of the principles upon which the Empire rested. To him it was such a visionary scheme that it bore no relation to practical politics.

In his early years, Laurier even assumed that separation, not centralization, was to be the fate of the Empire. He expected local autonomy gradually to be transformed into independence. But Laurier had no intention of hastening the process. Until English-Canadians and French-Canadians alike could accept independence, he was willing to suppress his view in the interest of racial harmony. [13] And in later years he more willingly accepted Canada's position within the Empire. Separation could be avoided by the preservation of autonomy in the future. It might be argued that this concept of the Empire was no more than the idea of independence in disguise. It seems a paradox to talk of countries being autonomous, and yet being part of an Empire, and it might appear that Laurier had resolved the paradox by accepting colonial bonds only when those bonds became meaningless. But this conclusion cannot be justified. Instead, to Laurier the Empire had a

[13] Public Archives of Canada, Lemieux Papers, I, Laurier to R. Lemieux, 1 Dec., 1892.

fundamental unity. To Laurier, the imperial connection was based
on the rather intangible bonds of a common political heritage and
common political ideals; yet these intangible bonds had concrete results
when imperial problems arose at the turn of the century. The British
Empire could have vitality even without contractual obligations.

Laurier's respect for British political traditions was an essential
part of his policy during the Boer War. From the beginning he was
convinced that the crisis in the Transvaal was of no concern to Canada.
He informed the press that the Canadian militia could not be sent off
to South Africa because the war was not being fought for the defence
of Canada and that, in any case, nothing could be done until Parliament was summoned to provide the money. [14] But these were only
pretexts. Like Sir John A. Macdonald in 1885, Laurier did not
believe it was his responsibility to help 'Chamberlain and Co.' out of
a hole. But when it became obvious that English-Canadians believed
that the Boer War was of direct concern to them, Laurier had to reconsider his decision. Again he was faced with an issue upon which the
two racial groups in Canada disagreed; again he sought a compromise
which would at least be acceptable to both groups. The Canadian
Government decided to recruit, equip and transport volunteers to
South Africa, with the Imperial Government assuming all subsequent
expenses.

It seems clear that the decision to send troops, although necessary
because of the danger of racial division, was possible for Laurier only
because he believed that the Boer War was a just war. With his
interest in political liberty and justice, it was natural for Laurier to
sympathize with the British subjects in the Transvaal. Months before
the war began, he had privately expressed to Governor General Minto
his strong sympathy for them. [15] To a more cynical correspondent,
he could state that, "To me it is clearly and manifestly a war for
religious liberty, political equality and civil rights." [16] In Parliament
he went so far as to state that he believed "there never was a juster war
on the part of England." [17] Since he believed this, the decision to
send troops could be determined by a consideration of Canadian
interests. Once he recognized that public feeling among English-
Canadians was strongly in favor of participation, Laurier was free to
accept participation in the interests of national unity. His confidence
in the honorable motives of British statesmen had made his decision an
easier one.

To illustrate the importance of Laurier's confidence in the British
sense of justice it is instructive to contrast his attitude with that of
Henri Bourassa. Bourassa agreed wholeheartedly with Laurier's original decision to keep out of the war. But when Laurier changed his
mind, Bourassa felt constrained to oppose his leader. Bourassa could
not credit British statesmen with such honorable motives as the desire
to defend political liberty. Instead, Bourassa saw the war as the result
of commercial imperialism; the natural result of the decline of British

[14] *Toronto Globe,* 4 Oct., 1899.
[15] Public Archives of Canada, Minto Papers, XX, 98, 2 May, 1899.
[16] Laurier Papers, 40865, W.L. to L. Gabriel, 6 Jan., 1900.
[17] Canada, House of Commons, *Debates,* 13 Mar., 1900, p. 1842.

industrial supremacy. [18]   Thus to Laurier the war was an isolated incident; to Bourassa it was the first of many such imperial wars. And so to Laurier, participation would eliminate a cause of friction between the two races in Canada; whereas to Bourassa, participation would set a precedent for future participation in imperial wars. Thus the disagreement between Laurier and Bourassa as to the British motives helps to account for the disagreement with respect to participation. If Laurier had not been an intellectual imperialist, with confidence in the justice of British diplomacy, it would have been difficult for him to accept participation in any form.

The same attitude can be seen in connection with Laurier's naval policy in 1910. Again Laurier would have preferred to avoid the question. At the Colonial Conference of 1902 he had refused to consider a direct contribution to the British Navy, explaining that his Government was "contemplating the establishment of a local naval force." [19]   In 1909 his Government was still contemplating. In that year, however, the German naval threat in Europe and the imperial sentiment roused by it in Canada ended the procrastination. The Naval Service Act of 1910 authorized a Canadian Navy, a navy which could only be placed on active service when the Governor in Council decided that a state of emergency had arisen; but a navy which could be placed at the disposal of the British Admiralty if the Canadian Government considered it advisable.

In this connection, the crucial point is whether Laurier expected this navy to become part of the British Navy in time of war. It seems clear that, in the event of a major war, he did. We may safely ignore his phrase, "When Great Britain is at war, Canada is at war", [20] since this was only a legal dictum and gave no guarantee of active participation in such a war. And yet, in spite of Laurier's well known aversion to the 'vortex of European militarism', he could agree with the more aggressive Canadian imperialists that British naval supremacy was desirable. And in a speech delivered in Montreal Laurier went even further and stated that Canada should support Great Britain when this naval supremacy was threatened.

> Nous ne sommes obligés de prendre part à aucune guerre, mais cependant je déclare que, s'il y avait des guerres — je ne veux pas Messieurs, d'équivoque sur ce point, — je suis ici pour défendre la politique que nous préconisons, s'il y avait une guerre dans laquelle la suprématie navale de l'Empire serait mise en péril, je serais d'opinion moi-même, — et je ne veux pas que d'autres en soient blâmés, parce que j'en prends la responsabilité — *je crois que nous devions aider l'Angleterre de toutes nos forces.* [21]

To understand fully the significance of this statement, it should be remembered that this speech was delivered in October, 1910, during the Drummond-Arthabaska by-election campaign, and was in fact Laurier's campaign speech. At this time Laurier was being denounced

[18] H. Bourassa, *Great Britain and Canada*, (Montreal, 1902), p. 27.
[19] *Colonial Conference, 1902, Minutes of Proceedings and Papers*, (London, 1902), p. 74.
[20] Canada, House of Commons, *Debates*, 12 Jan., 1910, p. 1735.
[21] A. D. DeCelles, ed., *Discours de Sir Wilfrid Laurier*, 1889-1911, (Montreal, 1920), p. 192, editor's italics.

by Bourassa and the *nationalistes* as an imperialist. Under these circumstances it is inconceivable that Laurier would have made such a provocative statement if he had not been sincere. Even though it was his policy, that he could make this statement at such a time suggests that Laurier had a quality considered rare among Canadian politicians, that he had the courage of his convictions.

Again the contrast between the attitude of Laurier and Bourassa illustrates how Laurier's respect for the political principles which Great Britain represented made possible the acceptance of an imperial role for the Canadian Navy. Bourassa still suspected the motives of the British leaders, and so believed that Laurier's policy would involve Canada in wars provoked by the Chamberlains and the Rhodes in England. [22] And so Bourassa could argue that the British Navy was no concern of Canada's; that Canada's only potential enemy was the United States, and that against the United States the British Navy would be of no protection. [23] But implicit in Laurier's policy was the assumption that Great Britain was the bastion of political liberty in the world, and that in a major war the British Navy would be defending the principle of political liberty rather than furthering British commercial interests. Hence Laurier was willing to commit Canada to the defence of British naval supremacy because the navy was a defence of British political principles in Canada too.

Laurier's attitude during the war of 1914-1918 is consistent with this point of view. In the special session of 1914, he reaffirmed his confidence in the motives of the British authorites by describing the war as being fought for freedom, for democracy, for civilization. [24] In 1916, to the suggestion that the war was luring Canada towards imperial federation, Laurier replied that "looking at it from the broader aspect, the triumph of Germany would be the triumph of Imperialism ten times aggravated by German *Kultur.*" [25] And even in 1917, when the war was increasing racial tensions in Canada to an alarming degree, Laurier was still able to argue that the various suggestions of a negotiated peace could not be accepted because such a settlement could not secure the principles for which the allies were fighting. [26] Had Laurier been an isolationist, he would surely have favored peace on almost any terms in 1917 in order to avert the conscription crisis. Even Laurier's attitude towards conscription was not inconsistent with this point of view. To Laurier, unity in Canada was still of paramount importance. He rightly believed that conscription would divide the country. Since conscription was unacceptable to the French-Canadians under any circumstances, it would be the negation of British political traditions to coerce them. The necessity of Canadian participation in the war was never questioned, but it should not be at the cost of sacrificing the political principles upon which the 'consolidation of Confederation' depended.

22 H. Bourassa, *Le Projet de loi navale*, (Montreal, 1910), p. 9.
23 *Ibid.*, p. 22.
24 Canada, House of Commons, *Debates,* 19 Aug., 1914, p. 9.
25 Laurier Papers, 192951, W.L. to J. Walsh, 31 Aug., 1916.
26 Laurier Papers, 194414, W.L. to W. Edwards, 11 Jan., 1917.

Thus our conclusion must be that Laurier was a moderate imperialist. On one occasion he wrote: "I have stated again and again that I was neither an Imperialist nor an anti-Imperialist: I am . . . a Canadian first, last and always." [27] But as a Canadian, vitally concerned with racial harmony in Canada, Laurier found in British liberal traditions the political principles upon which he believed the successful union of the two races could be achieved. To him, the Empire, and more specifically Great Britain, came to represent the bulwark of political liberty. For this reason he could and did oppose any schemes of imperial federation, since such centralization challenged the political liberty of the component parts of the Empire. But he was willing to condone Canadian participation in the Boer War because he saw it as a war to enforce political justice, and he was willing to rally to the defence of Great Britain in time of danger because he believed Great Britain would be defending the very political principles upon which the consolidation of Confederation depended. To this extent, Laurier was an imperialist.

[27] Laurier Papers, 196799, W.L. to F. Carrel, 24 Aug., 1917.

Goldwin Smith and Anti-Imperialism
CRAIG BROWN

IN THE LAST TWO YEARS of the nineteenth century Anglo-Saxondom, on both sides of the Atlantic, went to war. Significantly, in both cases, the cause of war was ostensibly just. The United States did battle with Spain to relieve Cubans living under the tortuous rule of a European monarch; Great Britain went to the relief of the oppressed Uitlanders on the Rand. Both wars were crusades, part of the "white man's burden," the necessary shedding of blood for the perpetuation (and expansion) of "Anglo-Saxon civilization."

The crusades were immensely popular throughout the North Atlantic community. One need only recall the magic of the "Rough Rider" to realize the reaction in the United States to the Spanish-American War. In England, John Morley noted with disgust the "hot levity with which even shrewd Liberals flung themselves into the Spanish-American struggle, and forgot the existence of a prudent and anti-Jingo sentiment in America."[1] Another British correspondent told Colonel Denison of Toronto that "we would not have countenanced a Cuba—say off the shores of Canada—for half the time the Yankees put up with it" and "it would be difficult to put a limit to the indignation which would have swept over this country if one of our men-of-war had been blown up like the Maine."[2] The response in Canada was equally enthusiastic. Sir Wilfrid Laurier received a flood of letters, poems, and songs praising the high purpose of America's venture into imperialism. One such song, for which Laurier offered polite thanks, contained the following verse:

> God guide our Cousins—o'er the Border!
> Rescue Cuba—in the fight,
> Trust in God, He'll help you conquer:
> Drive the Spaniards out of sight.[3]

[1]Cornell University, Goldwin Smith Papers, Morley to Smith, June 23, 1898.
[2]P.A.C., Denison Papers, 8, Murray to Denison, June 15, 1898.
[3]P.A.C., Laurier Papers, 77, #23994.

Reprinted from *Canadian Historical Review*, XLIII (2), June, 1962

The natural outcome of all this imperialistic fervour was renewed talk of an Anglo-Saxon alliance. Among its loudest proponents was the British Secretary of State for the Colonies, Joseph Chamberlain, who told a Birmingham audience in May, 1898, that "terrible as war may be, even war itself would be cheaply purchased if, in a great and noble cause, the Stars and Stripes and the Union Jack should wave together over an Anglo-Saxon alliance."[4] Morley reported that talk of an alliance brought "a fresh outburst of gush, under which the hard facts are completely submerged."[5] And a Canadian correspondent told Lord Salisbury that "Anglo-American Unity is a good thing to talk about just now, and following the English lead, our papers almost universally, as well as our public men in public utterances, are friendly to the States."[6]

From the isolation of the Grange in Toronto, Goldwin Smith spoke out with his usual vigour against the Anglo-Saxon alliance. "Alliance at this moment," Smith wrote to Morley, "means partnership with the party of war and aggrandizement now dominant at Washington."[7] When asked to join an Anglo-American committee, Smith curtly refused. "There seems to be something a little grotesque in a committee to organize friendship," he told Lord Rosebery. In any case, his association with such a group implied approbation "of a war which appears to me unjustifiable and frought [sic] with evil consequences to the American Commonwealth and the world."[8]

It was neither the committee nor even the Anglo-American alliance that bothered Smith. After all, Anglo-American union was a goal to which he had devoted most of his life and he described himself as "a thorough Anglo-American." Rather, it was the war that worried Smith. The "wretched war" completely disillusioned him; it was "in every way revolting."[9] The United States had been for Smith, "the hope of the English-speaking race."[10] Just before the war Smith wrote in the Weekly Sun, "The American Commonwealth is the greatest experiment ever made in popular government." With the advent of the Spanish-American War, the tense of the verb suddenly changed: "The American Republic was the hope of democracy."[11] "We are in

[4]Cited in L. M. Gelber, The Rise of Anglo-American Friendship: A Study in World Politics, 1898–1906 (London, 1938), 24. See also C. S. Campbell, Anglo-American Understanding, 1898–1903 (Baltimore, 1957), chap. 2.
[5]Smith Papers, Morley to Smith, June 23, 1898.
[6]Denison Papers, 8, Denison to Salisbury, June 12, 1898.
[7]Smith Papers, Smith to Morley, June 9, 1898.
[8]Ibid., Smith to Rosebery, July 11, 1898.
[9]A. Haultain, ed., Goldwin Smith's Correspondence (Toronto, n.d.), to John Cameron, June 2, 1898, and to Percy Bunting, June 21, 1898, pp. 315 and 319.
[10]F. H. Underhill, In Search of Canadian Liberalism (Toronto, 1960), 88.
[11]Cited in ibid., 100–1.

danger," Smith lamented, "of having the great industrial commonwealth turned into a filibustering war-power of the European type."[12]
The war, he believed, was the work of a "set of unprincipled politicians." In it he saw the destruction of "American Democracy." He
fully agreed with James Bryce that the American Constitution, the
American tradition, and the "political habits" of the Americans "seem
to unfit them for pursuing with success a great oceanic policy, perhaps
from governing well distant territories inhabited by inferior subject
races."[13] He was convinced that "the people" did not want war with
Spain but had been "mendaciously and wickedly" "maddened at the
critical moment" by the unscrupulous politicians at Washington.[14]

In the end, truth would conquer; the facts would be revealed and
McKinley and his friends would be turned out of the White House.
"There is a strong anti-Imperialist party, headed by the best men in
American public life," he told a friend in 1899, "the leaders of which
speak to me with great confidence of ultimate success."[15] Smith continually corresponded with many of the leading American anti-
imperialists, such as William Bourke Cockran and Carl Schurz. Though
he claimed to be no political tactician, in July, 1899, he advised the
latter not to hold public meetings of agitation: all that was necessary
was to present the facts to the people. "Let the facts speak for themselves to the popular intelligence." But, he added, he would not
arrest discussion. Instead, he would carry it "into the higher regions
of principle, showing . . . that if Imperialism and Militarism prevail,
'government of the people, by the people, for the people' will
'perish from the earth.' "[16]

The American anti-imperialists did not follow Smith's advice. As
early as November, 1898, the first Anti-Imperialist League was organized in Boston and in the following months the organization expanded
across the country, publicly voicing the sentiment of anti-imperialism
as it went.[17] But that was not of great importance. What was note-
worthy was that American anti-imperialists found support and en-
couragement for their ideas from men like Smith in Canada and
Bryce and Morley in England. Professor Osgood concludes that the
American anti-imperialists "fought with the complete assurance that
they were on the side of the Lord and the Declaration of Indepen-

[12]Smith Papers, Smith to Morley, June 9, 1898.
[13]Ibid., Bryce to Smith, July 6, 1898.
[14]Ibid., Smith to Rosebery, July 11, 1898.
[15]Haultain, ed., Correspondence, to Mrs. Hertz, November 9, 1899, p. 331.
[16]Smith Papers, Smith to Schurz, July 6, 1899. This same idea is expressed in New
York Public Library, Wm. B. Cockran Papers, Smith to Bourke Cockran, Nov. 10,
1899.
[17]F. H. Harrington, "The Anti-Imperialist Movement in the United States, 1898–
1900," Mississippi Valley Historical Review, XXII, 1935, 216.

dence; and, in the end, the imperialists proved no match for the spiritual might of their zealous adversaries. Indeed, the superior moral confidence of the anti-imperialists was not misplaced, for they were squarely in line with America's deep-rooted liberal and humane tradition."[18] To this Goldwin Smith would simply have added "Amen."

The South African War was an even greater shock to the anti-imperialists than the Spanish-American War had been. For Smith, the subjugation of the Boer republics was both a further stimulus to fight imperialism and a source of deeper disillusionment. As he prepared to sail to Italy in November, 1899, he wrote that he was "really glad to be at sea for the next ten days and to hear nothing of this vile war, which . . . has estranged me from my country."[19] "I doubt," Smith told J. X. Merriman, treasurer of the Cape Colony, "whether England has been put in a worse moral position since the burning of Joan of Arc."[20] And the enthusiastic response to the war in Canada made Smith even more sick at heart. "The brutal passions of this deplorable war," he lamented, are "made more brutal by colonial vulgarity. Most repulsive is the sight of Volunteers going . . . to slaughter people who have done them no wrong in a cause about which they know nothing."[21] But removal to the placid shores of the Mediterranean did not mean that Goldwin Smith had withdrawn from the battle. Week after week his little Toronto newspaper, the *Weekly Sun*, did combat with the imperially minded English-Canadian press.

The *Weekly Sun*, Smith thought, had an advantage over its adversaries and the cause it espoused was gaining ground. The advantage was his correspondence with Merriman which provided him with expert commentary from a man on the scene of action. "I have been putting forth the views which I hold in common with you, and in great measure on your authority," he reported to Merriman, adding that the paper "has been rapidly increasing its circulation."[22] That Merriman's reports on the war were transposed to Smith's paper was true, but his report of the results was mere wishful thinking. In fact, the *Weekly Sun's* stand on the South African War cost it nearly half its readers.[23]

Other background material for Smith's writing came from Bryce and Morley in England. In large measure this correspondence was devoted to the evil plots of Chamberlain, Milner, and Rhodes, and

[18]R. E. Osgood, *Ideals and Self-Interest in America's Foreign Relations* (Chicago, 1953), 49.
[19]Haultain, ed., *Correspondence*, to Mrs. Hertz, Nov. 9, 1899, p. 330.
[20]*Ibid.*, to Merriman, Dec. 1, 1899, p. 333.
[21]*Ibid.*, to Collins, Feb. 18, 1900, p. 343.
[22]*Ibid.*, to Merriman, Dec. 25, 1899, p. 334.
[23]E. Wallace, *Goldwin Smith, Victorian Liberal* (Toronto, 1957), 197.

particularly those of the Colonial Secretary. Like Smith, neither Bryce nor Morley lost any love on Chamberlain. Bryce had feared his "rashness" from the day he assumed office and believed that the South African War was "virtually the doing of Chamberlain." He believed that the anti-imperialist Liberals would even "be willing to purchase . . . a prolongation of Tory rule" by Chamberlain's retirement. It would be "the greatest good that could happen to British politics."[24] John Morley, older man that he was, was more inclined to dwell on the past and brood over the split of the Liberal party into its imperialist and anti-imperialist factions. "At the moment we are in the wilderness with a vengeance," he told Smith. "If we had such a man as Peel, backed by a man like Graham, we should have a better chance— to say nothing of Mr. G. The more I dig and delve, the higher my feeling for that breed, with Bright and Cobden among them."[25] Not only had English Liberalism lost its sense of direction, the whole idea of a "moral civilization" was regarded as "sickly cant" in Chamberlain's England. With deep remorse Morley could only observe that "many things went down into Mr. Gladstone's grave."[26]

Smith's activity was not confined simply to articles in the *Weekly Sun*. His voice was listened to more attentively by American anti-imperialists once the South African War had begun. This was particularly true in the case of William Bourke Cockran. Again and again Smith urged him to speak out against American imperialism in the Philippines and British imperialism in South Africa. Further, Smith believed that Cockran and his colleagues were allowing their opponents "an undue advantage in permitting them to use the term 'expansion' as they do. Expansion means extension without breach of continuity or loss of moral unity. Louisiana was expansion. Canada would be expansion. The Phillippines [*sic*] clearly are not."[27] Cockran followed Smith's suggestions practically to the letter. He told a Boston audience that "the pretense that the overthrow of the Transvaal Republic is essential to the growth of civilization is hardly worthy of discussion."[28] On the other hand, the students and faculty of the University of Michigan heard him say that:

Expansion in the American sense is not a new or untried political experiment. The fruits which it has borne prove that it is a policy of wisdom and justice. Its extension would promote the progress of civilization throughout the world. The expansion of this Republic to the frozen seas of the North would work immense benefit to the people of Canada, to the people of Great Britain, to the people

[24] Smith Papers, Bryce to Smith, May 18, 1896, and Nov. 4, 1899.
[25] *Ibid.*, Morley to Smith, Sept. 19, 1899.
[26] *Ibid.*, Morley to Smith, June 23, 1898.
[27] Cockran Papers, Smith to Cockran, Nov. 10, 1899.
[28] J. McGurrin, *Bourke Cockran* (New York, 1948), 201.

of the United States and to the whole human race. It would obviate all disputes about boundaries; it would prevent the unhuman, senseless destruction of the seal fisheries, and above all, it would abolish that system of customs taxation which impedes the free exchange of commodities, and therefore narrows the volume of production on both sides of the frontier.[29]

Undoubtedly this speech warmed the cockles of Smith's heart; it was simply a summation of *Canada and the Canadian Question.*

In March, 1900, Smith wrote to Cockran from Florence, Italy, asking if it was not possible "when the proper time comes, [to] pay some tribute to the memory of the Boers who have fallen fighting heroically not in their own cause alone, but in that of humanity?"[30] In May, Smith wrote from Toronto that when the Boers sued for peace, "it is obviously desirable that their appeal shall be so formed as to call forth the generous feelings of the British people, engage the sympathies of the world, and facilitate the work of the Liberals in England who will be combatting the policy of vengeance on which Chamberlain, Rhodes and the violent party are evidently bent." "Nobody," Smith told Cockran, "could frame such an appeal better than you can."[31] This idea was apparently passed over without comment by Cockran, but he did associate himself actively with the Boer envoys on their visit to the United States. They had an "enthusiastic reception" at Washington but Cockran feared that if they continued their American tour, their cause would become a party question in the 1900 election. He therefore thought it best that the Boers "leave these shores at once with a temperate statement of their cause, and a dignified expression of their disappointment that this great republic could not use its influence to save two weak but heroic republics from extinction by a powerful empire." Cockran also told Smith that the Boers expressed themselves in very "warm terms of your friendly attitude."[32]

In addition to his writings in the *Weekly Sun* and his suggestions to American anti-imperialists, Goldwin Smith also had to explain Canada's attitude to the South African War to his friends. He was glad to tell Cockran that "Toronto is the centre of Jingoism and almost its circumference. The same spirit by no means prevails in the country at large."[33] Merriman learned from Smith that "nine-tenths of the French Province were certainly the other way."[34] And with full approval he told Lord Mount Stephen that "anti-imperialism . . . is

[29]*Ibid.*, 194–5.
[30]Cockran Papers, Smith to Cockran, March 21, 1900.
[31]*Ibid.*, Smith to Cockran, May 18, 1900.
[32]Smith Papers, Cockran to Smith, May 22, 1900.
[33]Cockran Papers, Smith to Cockran, Nov. 10, 1899.
[34]Haultain, ed., *Correspondence*, to Merriman, Dec. 1, 1899, p. 334.

showing a strong front in Quebec, and Conservatives as well as Liberals are taking part."[35] As far as Laurier was concerned, Smith believed that he was "acting against his better judgment."[36] Smith contended that "pressure was put by Chamberlain through Lord Minto on Laurier to make him send the contingent."[37] This did not mean that Smith approved of Laurier's part in sending the Canadian contingent or even that he felt the Prime Minister was a innocent pawn in the hands of the imperialists. On the one hand, a forceful man would not have done Chamberlain's bidding; Laurier was "a good, but not a strong man."[38] On the other hand, and more important in Smith's mind, was the belief that Laurier himself had joined the imperialist camp.

At first Smith considered Laurier's victory in 1896 as "a defeat of Imperialism." But by May, 1897, he had changed his mind. After seeing the legislation of the first session of the Liberal Parliament he regretfully told a friend that "Mr. Laurier's government, after being for some time on the fence, has pretty evidently 'climbed down' on the Imperialist and anti-Continental side. It is pandering to the military spirit."[39] The result of the Imperial Conference and Jubilee of 1897 confirmed Smith's suspicion. Laurier, he wrote, "has been spoiled by the Jubilee, which was an Imperialist and militarist demonstration, and by his knighthood."[40] Just after the despatch of the second Canadian contingent to South Africa, Smith acidly observed that "titles have a terrible effect on colonial virtue."[41]

If Smith despaired of Laurier's surrender to imperialism, he was overjoyed at the stand taken by the young Liberal member for Labelle, Henri Bourassa. Bourassa had gained sudden prominence by his split with Laurier and his resignation from Parliament on the issue of sending a Canadian contingent to South Africa.[42] He told Smith, in January, 1900, that he thought it was his "duty to take a firm stand against the current of militarism and jingoism which is carrying public opinion in Canada." For this, Smith had granted him in one of his public letters " 'a certificate of good service.' " "It is to be hoped," added the master of the Grange, "that having put his hand to the plough, he will not turn back." Bourassa assured him that he would continue "tracing my humble furrow as straight as possible."[43]

Bourassa confessed that he had no delusions about stopping the

[35]Ibid., to Mount Stephen, March 12, 1900, p. 349.
[36]Ibid., to Merriman, Dec. 25, 1899, p. 335.
[37]Cockran Papers, Smith to Cockran, Nov. 10, 1899.
[38]Haultain, ed., Correspondence, to Merriman, Dec. 1, 1899, p. 334.
[39]Smith Papers, Smith to Wilson, June 25, 1896, and May 13, 1897.
[40]Haultain, ed., Correspondence, to Merriman, Dec. 25, 1899, p. 335.
[41]Ibid., to E. S. Beesly, Jan. 7, 1900, p. 339.
[42]See R. Rumilly, Henri Bourassa (Montreal, 1953), 52–4.
[43]Smith Papers, Bourassa to Smith, Jan. 20, 1900.

imperialist movement and that he had broken with Laurier even though he was "perfectly convinced that it' would bring me trouble, abuse and very little success." The young French Canadian was not bothered by "afterdate prophesies" that he had given up a "promising career." He believed that it was his "duty" to stand out against imperialism "whatever the consequences might be." As he said, "I have no care for power at the expense of all principles." At the same time, Bourassa took a kindlier view of Laurier's action than did Smith. He realized that the Prime Minister had acted from "a higher motive than personal ambition and self interest." Indeed, he believed that "the dread of creating a racial animosity between the French & English populations" had forced Laurier to "yield to the pressure of the jingo element." However, Bourassa did not share the Prime Minister's fear but believed that Laurier's action would promote tension between English- and French-speaking Canadians. "Don't you think," he asked Smith,

that these repeated concessions to the fear of racial animosity have simply the effect of developing that sentiment? Here is a liberal government, brought to power under the flag of national pacification and harmony. They are now going back on the oldest, the soundest, the most respectable principle of constitutional liberalism and playing in [to] the hands of Mr. Chamberlain and other megalomaniac imperialists—and this, because they are afraid of being called a french dominated and priest ridden government. Don't you think it is a direct premium offered to racial appeals?[44]

Smith agreed. "I have thought all along," he observed to Lord Mount Stephen, "that the effect of the Jingo policy would be, instead of sealing the union of races, to revive their division; and so it is."[45]

Smith and Bourassa kept up a close correspondence on the problem of imperialism. In May, 1900, the latter wrote that he had considered asking for a debate in the House of Commons on the proposed terms of peace with the Boer republics. But on "due reflection" he concluded the proper occasion had "not yet arisen." The jingo movement was "cooling down" but not yet enough "to inspire common sense and moral courage to our rulers." Even those who had been "annoyed" at Canada's participation in the South African War, he said, "would still be ready to manifest their loyalism by shouting: war to the bitter end!" In addition, "as our govt. seems to be more anxious to follow currents of opinion or even of prejudice rather than fight them, they would not hesitate in approving the position taken by Mr. Chamberlain. So that any debate raised on this question now would make our position

---

[44] *Ibid.*
[45] Haultain, ed., *Correspondence*, to Mount Stephen, March 12, 1900, p. 349.

worse."[46] As it was, when Bourassa raised the question of whether a
precedent had been created by sending the Canadian contingents, only
nine fellow Quebec M.P.'s supported him.[47]

Laurier's government had been elected in 1896. As early as November, 1899, the Prime Minister was thinking about the next election.[48]
An election would not be called until after the excitement of the
sending of the contingents had passed away, but it was clear that
Laurier and his party would have to go to the people either late in
1900 or early in 1901. With this in mind, Bourassa told Smith in May,
1900, that he was "studying quickly the best means that may be taken
to organize [the anti-imperialist] movement in a more substantial
form." In Quebec, he said, the feeling against imperialism was "strong,
though yet unsettled." And, he asked, "would it be possible to do
something in Ontario?"[49]

Smith was an old hand at organizing non-partisan political movements in Ontario. More than a decade before he had been the guiding
light of the Commercial Union movement. He had run headlong into
the solid Ontario wall of "loyalism," seen his plan watered down and
adopted by the Liberals as Unrestricted Reciprocity, and then watched
the masterful Sir John Macdonald carry the country as a dying "British
subject" in the 1891 election. Smith realized that the South African
War struck an even deeper chord in Ontario than had Macdonald's
appeal in 1891. The latter had been a curious mixture of British sentiment and Canadian nationalism; the former was a clear-cut case of
approval or disapproval of the British government's South African
policy. And apparently he advised Bourassa that a "more substantial"
anti-imperialist movement in Ontario was out of the question.

Bourassa replied that he recognized "the position in which the
anti-imperialists of Ontario are situated—especially when I realize
that in Quebec we are not so much better—in spite of the favourable
popular feeling." If the problem in Ontario was loyalism, in Quebec it
was the political acumen of Sir Wilfrid Laurier, who, Bourassa wrote,

. . . is likely to make a popular campaign in Quebec after the session. I imagine
he is going to paint Imperial Federation under its impossible colours and say
that he is opposed to that project. His followers and his organs will shout that
Laurier is more of a patriot and of a Canadian than ever and will thus induce
the people to believe that Laurier is an anti-imperialist. They will thus prevent

[46]Smith Papers, Bourassa to Smith, May 17, 1900.
[47]O. D. Skelton, *Life and Letters of Sir Wilfrid Laurier* (New York, 1922), II,
105–9.
[48]Laurier Papers, 129, Laurier to Ross, Nov. 10, 1899, and 133, Sifton to Laurier,
Dec. 10, 1899.
[49]Smith Papers, Bourassa to Smith, May 17, 1900.

the electors to realize [*sic*] that, whilst Sir Wilfrid is opposed to an impossible form of Federation, he is leading them to the real practical military imperialism. You know how hard it is to bring the masses and even the supposed educated men to appreciate future events and yet unapplied theories.

In addition, Bourassa admitted there were great difficulties facing the organization of a strong anti-imperialist movement. It would require "several men of talent, of good will and of strong character; it would require also good organs so as to make a thorough and effective press campaign, which means a good deal of money." "All of this," he sadly observed, "we lack."[50]

In spite of the obstacles, Bourassa was determined to carry on. "The little we can do," he said, "we shall do." With a general election coming on, he suggested several proposals to Smith. The anti-imperialists would try to force several of the candidates to sign a short and clear declaration against imperialism. He had heard from W. D. Gregory, a young admirer of Smith, that there was a strong anti-military sentiment in one of the Bruce constituencies where there was a large German-Canadian population. He noted that "if it were possible to pledge one of the candidates against future participation of Canada in foreign wars, it would be in itself a great success. It would destroy the argument that the movement is solely confined to the French-Canadians." Again, he believed that "the Irish clergy is generally opposed to the war and to imperialism in general." "Don't you believe," he asked, "something should be tried in Counties where there is a large Irish vote?"[51] In another letter, Bourassa said that the coming election had forced him to give up the anti-imperialist campaign in Quebec. He expected a "strong fight" in his constituency of Labelle, especially as a "jingo fund" had been raised in Ottawa to help defeat him. But as far as anti-imperialism was concerned, he thought he had "sown a seed which will produce some good later on. And I don't propose to let it die in the ground after the elections are over."[52]

Smith, too, turned his thoughts to the election. He was particularly concerned about Quebec. While it was true that "nine-tenths" of Quebec was opposed to the South African War, he believed that factor had to be "balanced by affection for a [French] Canadian Premier and his meal bag." In Ontario he believed that many Liberals were "offended by the failure of the Government to fulfil its election promises."[53] The turning out of the Liberals would not have been a disappointment to him. "A defeat of Laurier and the Pseudo-Liberal Imperialists would practically be the best thing that could happen,"

[50]*Ibid.*, Bourassa to Smith, July 12, 1900.
[51]*Ibid*
[52]*Ibid.*, Bourassa to Smith, Oct. 6, 1900.
[53]*Ibid.*, Smith to Mount Stephen, Aug. 31, 1900.

he told Cockran. "The straight Tories do us less harm, and the Pseudo-Liberals occupy the ground on which, if they were out of the way, something really liberal might be formed."[54] It was not that Smith trusted the Tories more; rather, he trusted the Liberals less. Indeed, he thought the Conservative party had little chance against Laurier because it did not have "better men." "It has nobody but old Tupper," he commented to Lord Mount Stephen, "who goes about bellowing like a bull without making much impression; and Foster, who is an able man and a good speaker but somehow has no hold upon the country. Young Tupper has failed, and Hugh John Macdonald, whom they are trying to push to the front, has nothing but his father's name."[55]

Smith's wish that the "Pseudo-Liberals" would be turned out of office did not come true. As the Governor General, Lord Minto, said to his brother, the 1900 election "was a tremendous victory for Sir Wilfrid." "Too much so," Minto added, "all the opposition leaders having been beaten and he is anything but in good spirits about it."[56] Laurier himself confessed his fears about his triumph in a note to Lord Aberdeen. "I could well wish," he wrote, "our victory had not been as complete as it is. I would rather have a strong opposition in the house, with able men to lead it, than to have, in face of us, simply a mob with ward politicians at the head of it."[57] Old Sir Charles Tupper was gone; and so were George Foster and the young white hope of the Conservative party, Hugh John Macdonald.

More important for Smith than the defeat of the Conservatives was the apparent vindication of all Laurier's policies, including Canada's part in the South African War. The turn of the tide in the war and the return of the Conservatives in the British general election also weakened Smith's position. The fate of the Boer republics was sealed; though it would take time, they eventually would be destroyed. In short, if anti-imperialism in Canada was not losing ground, it was not gaining ground either. And this was evident in the change of mood of Goldwin Smith. He had invited Frederic Harrison to visit the Dominion but added that there was not "anything very bright or comforting in Canada to show you." "I will not say that I have been crying in the wilderness," Smith wrote, "but I have been crying in an apparent wilderness." His "little organ," the *Weekly Sun*, "and a still smaller organ," the *Bobcaygeon Independent*, were the only two English-Canadian journals opposed to the war. Even worse, though

54Cockran Papers, Smith to Cockran, Oct. 14, 1900.
55Smith Papers, Smith to Mount Stephen, Aug. 31, 1900.
56P.A.C., Minto Papers, 36, Minto to Elliot, Nov. 25, 1900.
57P.A.C., Aberdeen Papers, 3, Laurier to Aberdeen, Dec. 1, 1900.

there was "a certain amount of feeling on our side . . . it is cowed and silent."[58]

Still, Smith and Bourassa would continue to fight the good fight. The latter had said he would not let die the seed he had planted in Quebec. The former was "not without hope of an approaching reaction" against imperialism.[59] And both did carry on their battle to the end of their days. Yet Bourassa and Smith did not join their forces to create an anti-imperialist organization such as the League south of the border. Ostensibly their goal was the same: condemnation of the high-handed policy of Chamberlain and the prevention of Canada's participation in foreign wars. Bourassa had in fact suggested organizing the "movement in a more substantial form." But Smith had spurned the idea in mid-1900 and it was not taken up again. Why? In part it was probably true that Bourassa had his eye on the 1900 general election and that both he and Smith agreed that neither sufficient talent nor money could be found in time. But there appear to be other more fundamental reasons why a "more substantial form" of organization would have failed.

In the first place, it is hardly possible that Bourassa had forgotten the sharp rebuke his fellow French Canadians had received in Smith's *Canada and the Canadian Question*. If anything, Smith had spoken more harshly of French Canada than had Lord Durham a half century earlier. To Smith's mind French Canada was the cause of Canadian political corruption; it was an "uncommercial" province, a "nonconductor between the more commercial members of the Confederation"; it was a "separate nation" which must be "ultimately absorbed in the English-speaking population of a vast Continent."[60] Nor had Smith's opinion of French Canada changed greatly in the years since he had written *Canada and the Canadian Question*. French-Canadian politicians "are loyal to the loaves and fishes of Ottawa," he told a friend, "loyal to Great Britain they never were."[61] True, Bourassa might be an exception to the loyalty to "loaves and fishes," but the election of 1900 only proved how great an exception he was. And Bourassa would hardly have agreed with Smith's solution of the problem, the absorption of French Canada.

Secondly, Goldwin Smith drew a fine distinction between "imperialism" and "expansion" which Bourassa could not possibly have accepted. Expansion meant "extension without break of continuity or loss of moral unity"; imperialism was, then, extension where continuity was lost and moral unity was broken. And at the very same

[58]Haultain, ed., *Correspondence*, to Harrison, Dec. 9, 1900, p. 365.
[59]*Ibid.*
[60]G. Smith, *Canada and the Canadian Question* (Toronto, 1892), 244.
[61]Smith Papers, Smith to Mowbray, Feb. 7, 1898.

time that Smith battled against imperialism he continued to urge the peaceful annexation of Canada to the United States. In June, 1900, he wrote to Cockran, who had risen to a position of considerable influence in the Democratic party, that the question of Canadian annexation "should be left in the hands of the Democratic Convention and its leaders."[62] A short while later he urged that written into the Democratic platform at the Kansas City convention should be "a declaration in favour of genuine expansion, that is to say the free and peaceful Union of this Continent, in opposition to the subjugation of distant countries and alien races."[63] This was the cause to which Smith devoted his life. Annexation would break down the unnatural trade barrier across the continent, it would further the unity of Anglo-Saxondom, and incidentally, it would solve the French-Canadian problem. A decade earlier he had written that British Canada alone would always have to put up with Quebec, but with annexation the French Canadians would ultimately be overwhelmed.[64]

Bourassa made a more sweeping condemnation of imperialism. He believed that the "imperialist frenzy . . . is the result of a perverted social education. The worship of gold, of stock gambling, of purely material ideals by the individuals develop a national instinct of abnormal expansion . . . and brings naturally the military frenzy which is the means of grabbing and maintaining foreign territory." This, he thought, was certainly true of Great Britain. And he was not willing to credit the United States with the ability to draw a line between the "imperialist frenzy" and peaceful expansion. "Don't you think," he asked Smith, "that our neighbours are more than emulating their cousins of the old world?"[65] More than that, annexation of Canada, whether it came with expansionist pamphlets or imperialist guns, meant the extinction of French Canada. And he was determined to preserve French Canada within a Canadian nation.

Because of this the anti-imperialism of Henri Bourassa and the anti-imperialism of Goldwin Smith could follow parallel lines and there could even be a co-operative exchange of correspondence between the two men, but the two lines could never meet. The movement could not take on a "more substantial form." Smith and Bourassa could condemn the Spanish-American War and the South African War. But Smith's "genuine expansion" would have been imperialism to Bourassa; peaceful imperialism, yes, but still imperialism. Smith would have retorted, as he did in *Canada and the Canadian Question*, that it was "the step of Destiny."[66]

[62]Cockran Papers, Smith to Cockran, June 13, 1900.
[63]*Ibid.*, June 23, 1900.
[64]Smith, *Canada and the Canadian Question*, 237.
[65]Smith Papers, Bourassa to Smith, Oct. 6, 1900.
[66]Smith, *Canada and the Canadian Question*, 346.

Sir Wilfrid Laurier and Lord Minto

H. PEARSON GUNDY

IN *Laurier: a Study in Canadian Politics* (1922) the late Mr. John W. Dafoe, without benefit of supporting documents, made a strong indictment of Lord Minto as Governor-General, an indictment repeated and embroidered by many later writers.

"Laurier had five years of more or less continuous struggle with Lord Minto, a combination of country squire and heavy dragoon, who was sent to Canada in 1898 to forward by every means in his power the Chamberlain policies. He busied himself at once and persistently in trying to induce the Canadian Government to commit itself formally to the policy of supplying Canadian troops for Imperial wars . . . With the outbreak of the South African War Lord Minto regarded himself less as Governor-General than as Imperial Commissioner charged with the vague and shadowy powers which go with that office; and Sir Wilfrid had, in consequence, to instruct him on more than one occasion that Canada was still a self-governing country and not a military satrapy . . . The story which would be most interesting and suggestive, will perhaps never be told."[1]

Part of the story was told in very different terms two years later by John Buchan in *Lord Minto, a Memoir.* In the eighty odd pages dealing with Minto's Canadian sojourn, from November 1898 to November 1905, Buchan presents the relations of the Governor-General to his First Minister in a light more favourable to both men. Each shrewdly assessed the other, and respected the other's integrity; by frank speaking they agreed to differ or composed their differences. Yet the charges of interference on the part of Minto, of jingoistic imperialism, disrespect for constitutional practice, and irritable stubbornness are repeated by Creighton,[2] Lower,[3] Penlington[4] and others.

The Minto-Laurier correspondence, formerly at Queen's and now in the Public Archives, supplemented by lately acquired transcripts of the Minto Papers, also in the Archives, dispel the myth of squire-cum-dragoon and reveal Minto as a shrewd constitutional governor whose services to Canada have received scant recognition. Skelton, who knew the documents, could have given just credit to Minto. But apart from two or three passing references, he relegates him to a footnote in which he quotes Laurier's conversational comment: "Lord Minto had much sound sense, a stronger man than was thought.

[1] John W. Dafoe, *Laurier: A Study in Canadian Politics,* (Toronto, 1922), 78-79.

[2] Donald G. Creighton, *Dominion of the North: A History of Canada,* (Boston, 1944), 399-400.

[3] Arthur R. M. Lower, *Colony to Nation: A History of Canada,* (Toronto, 1946), 400, 443.

[4] Norman Penlington, "General Hutton and the Problem of Military Imperialism in Canada, 1898-1900" (*Canadian Historical Review,* XXIV, June, 1943, 156-171).

Reprinted from Canadian Historical Association, *Report,* 1952

When he came to Canada first he was absolutely untrained in constitutional practice, knew little but horses and soldiering, but he took his duties to heart and became an effective governor, if sometimes very stiff."[5]

The suggestion that Minto was Chamberlain's protégé is supported by neither Buchan nor Garvin[6]. The Colonial Secretary's choice had been the Duke of Connaught but the Queen had withheld her consent. It was only after several other distinguished nominees had declined the post, that Chamberlain consented to Minto, put forward by Lord Wolseley. Although he lacked political experience, his strength lay in a first-hand knowledge of imperial problems from military service in Afghanistan, in Egypt, and in Canada as Chief of Staff to General Middleton during the North West Rebellion. While his views on the Empire coincided more closely with those of Chamberlain than with those of Laurier, he was without taint of jingoism, and before coming to Canada had been critical of Chamberlain's policy in South Africa.[7]

On assuming office, Minto was immediately attracted to Laurier, "Far the biggest man in Canada",[8] and subtly appreciated what he called the "honourable opportunism" by which he united the support of both sections of the population. Minto never underestimated the difficulties that beset his Prime Minister, least of all at the time of the South African War.

Preoccupied with the Manitoba School Question, the opening up of the West, railway policy, and Canadian-American relations, Laurier had not followed closely events in the Transvaal. Britain was conducting various skirmishes in India, in Egypt, on the Afghan border, in Hong-Kong, in which Canadian participation was not even mooted. Trouble in South Africa seemed just as remote, a menace neither to the Empire nor to Canada. To the Canadian imperialists, however, both Liberal and Tory, the situation, already grave, was in danger of becoming much worse. Publication of the Uitlanders' petition to the Queen for redress of their grievances stirred imperial fervor, and there was talk in Ottawa of introducing a resolution of sympathy with these disfranchised British subjects.

As soon as Minto learned of this, on May 2, 1899, he wrote to Laurier: "I yesterday heard indirectly there was some idea here of asking me to recommend an expression of sympathy from Canada with the Uitlanders in South Africa. I hear something has already been said to you about it. I feel sure you will agree with me, viz, I am decidedly of opinion that it would be very inopportune at present to mingle in any way with South African complications. There may be plenty of opportunity later on to show our good will — but at present we do not even know what line the Imperial Government may adopt."[9]

[5]Oscar D. Skelton, *Life and Letters of Sir Wilfrid Laurier*, (2 vols., Toronto, 1921), II, 86 n.
[6]John L. Garvin, *The Life of Joseph Chamberlain*, (London, 1924), vol. III.
[7]John Buchan, *Lord Minto: A Memoir*, (London, 1924), 105.
[8]*Ibid.* 159.
[9]Public Archives of Canada, Laurier Papers. (*Note*: At the time of writing, the Laurier Papers formerly at Queen's University are in process of being interfiled with those previously deposited in the Public Archives. New volume numbers have not yet been assigned.)

The 'line' was soon clarified. On July 3, Chamberlain sent a "secret and confidential" message to Minto asking if Canada would volunteer troops in event of war but without the application of "external pressure or suggestion".[10]

By mid-July, when Minto received the letter, Kruger was making some concessions and Britain had held out the 'olive branch' of a joint inquiry into the franchise proposals. As it appeared that the crisis might be averted, it was not the most opportune time to sound out Laurier on the question of contributing troops. "The news this morning looks rather better," Minto wrote to him, "but it is quite possible it is only the lull before the storm. and no doubt the greater show of strength the Empire can now make, the better are the chances of peace."[11] Had the Prime Minister considered the possibility of Canada's offering troops? Such an offer should be spontaneous, "not merely the result of a desire to meet hopes expressed at home". As an old friend of Canada, Minto hoped that she might be first in the field.

Minto had to report to Chamberlain that, in the face of Quebec opposition, Laurier did not choose to compete in the race for offering troops. Nevertheless he assured the Colonial Secretary that "in any real emergency the British determination to assist the mother country will be irresistible by any government".[12]

A British agent from the South African League who had come to Canada to represent to the government the disabilities suffered by the Uitlanders, convinced Laurier that their cause was just. The Prime Minister now personally moved a resolution of sympathy with the efforts of Her Majesty's government to obtain justice for the Uitlanders, expressing the hope that "wiser and more humane counsels [would] prevail in the Transvaal and possibly avert the awful arbitrement of war".[13] Seconded by Mr. Foster, in the absence of Sir Charles Tupper, the resolution carried unanimously.[14]

To make his own position clear, Laurier, in forwarding the resolution to Minto, repeated his conviction that the colonies should not, in event of war, be asked by Britain or even expected to assume military burdens except in the case of pressing danger. Minto at once replied that "there has been no question of England asking for aid in troops, and no expression of opinion in any way that she considered herself justified in expecting such assistance . . . You know my own views on the question, but I quite recognize the serious considerations connected with such an offer.[15]

Despite the increasing tension as Kruger temporized and Britain prepared a seven-fold ultimatum, Minto would not and could not force the hand of the Canadian government. He had made his representations to Laurier, and Laurier had not changed his stand. Each respected the other's convictions. On September 28, Minto wrote to his brother, Arthur: "From the point of view of a Canadian statesman I don't see why they should commit their country to the expen-

[10]*Ibid.*
[11]*Ibid.*
[12]Garvin, *Joseph Chamberlain*, III, 530.
[13]Skelton, *Sir Wilfrid Laurier*, II, 92.
[14]Canada, *House of Commons Debates*, L (1899), 8994.
[15]Skelton, *Sir Wilfrid Laurier*, II, 92-93.

diture of lives and money for a quarrel not threatening imperial safety
and directly contrary to the opinion of a colonial government at the
Cape. They are loyal here to a degree . . . but I confess I doubt the
advisability of their taking part now, from the point of view of the
Canadian Government."[16]

Meanwhile the sands were running out in South Africa while
Kruger was preparing his ultimatum to forestall Chamberlain's. On
the eve of hostilities, August 3, the Colonial Secretary cabled the
colonies a message of thanks for the offer of troops, with detailed instructions for the organization of military units. Canada, of course,
had made no offer but Minto received a cable in identical terms, the
gist of which was published in *The Times* and reprinted in the Canadian press. By coincidence, on the same day that the cable was sent,
the *Canadian Military Gazette* announced without authorization that
the government would offer a contingent for South Africa. Sir
Wilfrid promptly denied the report as a pure invention. War had
not yet been declared; South Africa was not a menace to Canada;
parliament was in recess; no grant had been made, and no contingent
offered. "Though we may be willing to contribute troops", he said
to *The Globe* reporter, "I do not see how we can do so."[17]

Minto, who was in New York on October 5 when Chamberlain's
cable arrived, wrote to Laurier in obvious concern. The cabinet was
placed in the embarrassing position of being thanked for an offer that
had not been made, and of appearing niggardly and unpatriotic if
they did not equip a volunteer force out of public funds. His first
assurance was that the Colonial Secretary had certainly not intended
to embarrass the government; the cable could have reference only to
private offers, especially that of Col. Hughes. Nevertheless there
would be strong public reaction and an official reply would have to
be made. The offer of a contingent would more accord with public
sentiment. It might therefore be better "to reconsider the question
rather than to allow an irresponsible call for volunteers." "I can
not," he added, "think it advisable that Colonel Hughes should be
allowed to raise an expedition on his own responsibility representing
Canada."[18]

Before Laurier could consult with Minto, he had to leave Ottawa,
August 7, to keep an engagement with President McKinley in Chicago.
"For three days," says Willison, who accompanied the Prime Minister,
"we discussed the Imperial obligation of Canada and the possible
political consequences of a decision against sending contingents in all
its phases. . . Sir Wilfrid contended the war in South Africa . . .
would be a petty tribal conflict in which the aid of the Dominion
would not be required, and . . . over and over again he declared he
would put all the resources of Canada at the service of the mother
country in any great war for the security and integrity of the
Empire."[19]

While they were returning by train to Canada, the news broke
on August 11, that Britain had rejected the Boer ultimatum and war
had been declared. Laurier, "very sober and silent", pondered the

[16]Buchan, *Minto*, 136 n.
[17]Skelton, *Sir Wilfrid Laurier*, II, 93.
[18]*Ibid.* 94.
[19]Sir John Willison, *Reminiscences Political and Personal* (Toronto, 1919), 303.

consequences for Canada. Before leaving the train at Toronto, Willison urged him to issue an immediate announcement that the government would send troops; but the Prime Minister remained "reluctant, unconvinced, and rebellious".[20]

In Ottawa Sir Wilfred faced a divided council. Some, including Dr. Borden, the Minister of Militia, wanted a full Canadian contingent at government expense; others advocated unofficial volunteer units; the French-Canadians led by J. Israel Tarte wanted no share in Britain's wars without a voice in her foreign policy. At the end of the first day no agreement was reached and Minto cabled to Chamberlain that he saw no hope for a Canadian contingent.[21] The cabinet sat again on the 13th and after an all-day session reached a compromise. Without summoning parliament the government undertook to equip volunteers up to one thousand men and provide for their transportation to South Africa, on the understanding that this would not be "construed as a precedent for future action."[22]

Minto wrote at once to the Colonial Secretary clarifying Laurier's position. Public pressure, he felt, especially since the publication of Chamberlain's cable, had decided the issue. Laurier admitted "the undoubted necessity of war" but on grounds of policy was disinclined to admit that Canada should assume imperial liabilities. The point, however, had been minimized by the British offer to transport and pay Canadian troops. The Prime Minister, he assured Chamberlain, "is thoroughly imperialistic, though he may have his doubts as to colonial action. I like him very much. He takes a broad view of things, and has an extremely difficult team to drive . . . Quebec is perfectly loyal, but you cannot on such an occasion expect Frenchmen to possess British enthusiasm or thoroughly to understand it . . . I have myself carefully avoided any appearance of pressing for troops, but I have put what I believe to be the imperial view of the question strongly before Sir Wilfrid . . . "[23] Within two weeks the first Canadian contingent was ready to sail from Quebec, followed a few months later by a second.

The despatch of troops by Canada brought up the question of Canada's position when the war should end. On March 16, Senator Drummond took the opportunity of sounding out the Governor-General on the advisability of a resolution in the House claiming representation for Canada in the final peace negotiations.[24] Minto's reaction was favourable, though he felt that the resolution should not be expressed as a demand. If granted, it might lead to official Canadian representation in Britain's counsels as advocated by Tarte and Bourassa. He made it very clear to Drummond, however, that this was "absolutely private and not official advice in any way."[25] When he broached the matter to the Prime Minister, Minto was told in a very forthright manner that Sir Wilfrid "would not advise any such resolution, that he considered it very unadvisable—the country not [being] at present ripe for discussion of the question." As for

[20]*Ibid*, 304.
[21]Buchan, *Minto*, 140.
[22]Skelton, *Sir Wilfrid Laurier*, II, p. 97.
[23]Buchan, *Minto*, 141,. By "imperialistic" Minto seems to mean in this context "loyal in support of the British Empire".
[24]Public Archives of Canada, Minto Papers, Memorandum, 16 March, 1900.
[25]*Ibid*.

Tarte and Bourassa, they did not really want a closer imperial connection, but were content with things as they were, while "entertain-
ing the possibility of founding an independent French [Canadian]
republic."[26]

Canadian participation in the South African War directed public
attention to the whole subject of Canada's defence policy. Before the
war the Canadian army had been a toy command taken seriously
neither by the government nor by the War Office. The Permanent
Force numbered less than one thousand men; it was poorly equipped,
poorly paid, and commissions were bartered as minor patronage for
political services. The appointment of minister of militia was not
one of senior cabinet rank; at least since the days of Sir George Cartier.
Under the minister of militia and responsible to him was the G.O.C.
who, according to statute, had to be an officer in Her Majesty's regular
army not below the rank of colonel. Their respective spheres of influence were ill defined, however, and there was no body of precedent
as a safeguard against disagreement.

Sir Wilfrid Laurier's Minister of Militia, Dr. Frederick Borden,
a general practitioner from Nova Scotia, was both an ardent militia
man and an equally ardent politician. As minister he was determined
to 'Liberalize' the army, too long under Tory domination. Ancient
staff officers were retired, tenure of commands limited to five years,
annual camps instituted, and party followers induced to join the
reserve forces. Major-General Gascoigne, his G.O.C., spent most of
his time keeping up with the paper work that Borden's reorganization
entailed, and was glad to be relieved of the post in 1898. The Imperial authorities, having decided that an energetic officer was required
in view of South African complications, appointed Major-General E.
T. H. Hutton a few months before Minto became Governor-General.
The almost simultaneous appointment to Canada of two well known
military men appeared to augur a shake-up in the Canadian militia.
Before Minto left England, Hutton wrote to him, welcoming his assistance, but advising him to say nothing about militia reform until he
had acquainted him with the position of army affairs.[27]

According to Hutton's own unpublished account of his relations
with Minto, the Governor-General, while acting strictly in accord
with his constitutional rights, cooperated with the G.O.C. in educating public opinion and "by a combination of tact and firmness"
induced the government to adopt a policy formerly repudiated.[28]

Tact and firmness soon had to be exercised by Minto in a clash
between Hutton and Borden. Far from admiring the Minister's
vaunted reforms, the new G.O.C. was deeply shocked by the state of
the military establishments from coast to coast, and the ubiquitous
evidence of political interference. It was obvious that these colonials
needed an imperial officer to show them how an army should be run.
Everything was wrong, but everything would be put right; the public
must be informed and the nation must gird up its loins. The more
Hutton spoke, the more publicity he got, and the more he irritated the

[26]*Ibid*, Memorandum, 23 March, 1900.
[27]*Ibid*, Hutton to Minto, 9 November, 1898.
[28]Ibid, Sir E. T. H. Hutton, "Narrative of Lord Minto's Career" (Typescript,
Chapters 1 and 2 only.)

Minister of Militia who felt he was being made to appear responsible
for the deplorable state of the Canadian army. Minto took alarm and
wrote to Laurier "To tell you the truth I am very anxious he
[Hutton] should avoid public speaking and I have told hom so."[29]

Minor friction over promotions and commissions flared up when
Hutton innocently recommended a Conservative to replace Col.
Domville, a Liberal M.P. with a poor army record, already slated for
retirement. Hutton then wrote a personal letter to his Minister discussing some of their points of disagreement. Borden took the letter
to Laurier who sent it to Minto stating that it was his painful duty
to bring before His Excellency the conflict that had arisen between
General Hutton and the Minister of Militia.[30] Minto lectured Hutton
on his want of tact, and then in a long talk with Borden assured him
that the General wished to serve him well and give due credit for any
reforms to the Department. If Borden insisted upon reinstating Col.
Domville the G.O.C.'s position would be rendered quite untenable.
Concerning the offending letter, he wrote to Laurier, "I can not see
anything in the tone of it from beginning to end to which anyone
could take exception. It of course expresses differences of opinion
with Borden but beyond that it does not appear to go."[31] Ruffled
tempers were smoothed for the time being. and Hutton worked fever-
ishly to prepare the army for the possible emergency of service in
South Africa. Indeed the Cabinet began to suspect that he had secretly promised a Canadian contingent. For one thing, he discouraged
individual offers to volunteer; and he was totally opposed to Col. Sam
Hughes's campaign to raise a volunteer brigade. It was strongly
suspected later that Hutton had inspired the premature announcement
about a contingent in the *Canadian Military Gazette*. There is no
proof that he did, but certainly without his advance preparations the
first contingent could not so promptly have left Canada.

In organizing the second contingent, Hutton had another alter-
cation with Borden who suspected him of favouring Conservative
horse-dealers in purchasing horses for the mounted infantry. A
Liberal member was detailed to report on the General's purchasing
committee.

"I am truly and deeply sick at heart over this militia," Hutton
wrote to Minto, January 4, 1900. "It seems impossible to evolve
order out of chaos and to make dirty water run clear when the political
atmosphere polutes everything and no one goes for the public good."[32]

From the government point of view, Laurier informed Lord
Strathcona that Hutton was "meddlesome, ignores the authority of the
Minister and constantly acts as one who holds himself independent
of Civil Authority."[33]

The axe fell when Borden discovered that Hutton had given
orders to Col. Aylmer, the Adjutant-General, and Col. Foster, the
Quarter-Master General, not to see the Minister of Militia or show

[29]Laurier Papers, Minto to Laurier, 8 November, 1899.
[30]*Ibid*, Laurier to Minto, June, 1899. Cited by Penlington, *C.H.R.* XXIV,
June, 1943, 162 n.
[31]Laurier Papers, Minto to Laurier, 7 June, 1899.
[32]Minto Papers, Hutton to Minto, 24 January, 1900.
[33]Laurier Papers, Laurier Scrapbook, Feb. 1,. 1900, Very Confidential. Cited
by Penlington, *C.H.R.* XXIV, June, 1943, 167.

him any papers without permission of the G.O.C. and that all interviews must be reported to him.

All Minto's tact and firmness could not save the General from recall. But to state, as Penlington does,[34] that the interviews between Minto and Laurier over this episode were "heated and stormy" is to mistake the temper and tactics of both men. The clash between Hutton and Borden was not repeated by Minto and the Prime Minister. Minto, to be sure, was firm in protesting against political interference in purely military matters; Laurier was equally firm in maintaining that the G.O.C. was clearly subordinate to the Minister of Militia. When His Excellency suggested that a reshuffle of the cabinet might clear the air, Laurier replied that no minister except himself would agree to serve with General Hutton.[35] At the Prime Minister's request, Minto sent to him a confidential memorandum embodying the points which they had discussed, with a covering note in which he said "I am sure you know my views generally and will not say more, except that I am always most anxious to support you and sincerely wish a way could be found out of this troublesome business".[36]

A week later Minto was informed that the cabinet had issued for his signature an Order-in-Council asking for Hutton's recall. He accepted the decision, but in a note to Laurier stated that in forwarding the order "I shall feel bound to send with it a despatch in the general sense of the confidential memo I have already submitted to you".[37]

Laurier was not pleased. "At the drawing room in the evening," Minto wrote," . . . Sir Wilfrid Laurier seemed very stiff toward Her Excellency and me."[38] Next day the Prime Minister ill-advisedly broke a confidence by placing the Governor-General's memorandum before council. After the meeting Israel Tarte informed Lady Minto of Laurier's action which he considered very unfair to His Excellency.[39]

Minto wrote a pained rebuke to Laurier, but so couched as to avoid any breach in their relations.

"We have always so generally agreed in our views that I am very sorry to differ at all with you on any point, but for the sake of the position I have taken up I must repeat that the 'confidential memo' I sent to you was never intended to be laid before Council . . . though it embodied my conversation with you to a great extent, it was so worded that I am afraid Dr. Borden may have taken my words more to heart than would have been at all necessary from reading a more carefully prepared document. I have particularly wished to avoid creating any bitter feelings by anything I have said that might go beyond ourselves."[40]

After receiving this note, Laurier called at Government House with the privy council order which Minto signed. "He also" recorded Minto, "brought back my 'confidential memo' to himself which he had presented to council; he apologized very nicely for having done so and tore it up in my presence to be considered as never written."[41]

[34]Penlington, 167.
[35]Minto Papers, Memorandum, 31 January, 1900.
[36]Laurier Papers, Minto to Laurier, 20 January, 1900.
[37]*Ibid*, Minto to Laurier, 27 January, 1900.
[38]Minto Papers, Memorandum, January, 1900.
[39]*Ibid.*
[40]Laurier Papers, Minto to Laurier, 2 February, 1900.
[41]Minto Papers, Memorandum, 4 February, 1900.

One point which Minto had emphasized during this dispute was the need for defining more accurately the respective spheres of the G.O.C. and the Minister of Militia. The position, he pointed out to council, was rapidly becoming "such as a high minded British officer would not care to accept".[42] Laurier's reply was that all G.O.C.'s had failed because "they did not understand their constitutional position i.e. below the Minister. When they are appointed here, they come as Canadian officials not Imperial officers".[43]

Hutton's successor, Major General R. H. O'Grady Haly was merely a temporary appointment. The "high minded" British officer who finally accepted the post in 1902 was Major General the Earl of Dundonald. No sooner had Dundonald become G.O.C. than the politico-military pot was set boiling again.

On the second day after the General's arrival Laurier concluded an interview with him by saying "You must not take the Militia seriously, for though it is useful for suppressing internal disturbances, it will not be required for the defence of the country, as the Munroe doctrine protects us against enemy aggression."[44]—or so Dundonald reports him as saying. But the General was determined to make the government take the army seriously and stop playing politics with it. On each inspection tour he accumulated evidence of political interference, lists of Liberal tradesmen who had to be patronized, broken windows in a drill hall which could not be repaired until the Liberal glazier recovered from an illness, and so on. The organization of a new regiment in the Eastern Townships was held up for months because the Liberal Member, the Hon. Sidney Fisher, Minister of Agriculture, had to screen the list of commissions. When a final revised list was submitted for gazetting, Fisher, acting for the Minister of Militia who was away from Ottawa, scratched out the name of Dr. Pickel.

This was too much for Dundonald. In a speech to the officers of the District Militia in Montreal on June 4, 1904, he cited Fisher's action as "a gross instance of political interference" and an example of "extraordinary lack of etiquette".[45] Four days later the speech was reported in the *Ottawa Citizen* under the caption *A Military Sensation*. Next day a question was asked in the House which precipitated an acrimonious debate. There were charges and counter charges, egregious puns about "a tempest in a pickel pot", sharp exchanges between the leaders of both parties, and a dignified explanation by Laurier of his slip of the tongue in referring to Dundonald as a "foreigner" when he meant "stranger".

The G.O.C. placed his defence in the hands of the Hon. Sam Hughes whose long-winded speeches were characterized by a Liberal member as "a medley of blatherskite and rhodomontade" and the speaker himself as "the redoubtable only one genuine heaven-born, heaven-descended child of the gods—Sam Hughes".[46] The opposition retorted by calling Fisher a "chicken fattener" and Borden "a little tin god".

[42]*Ibid.*
[43]*Ibid.*
[44]Lieut.-Gen. The Earl of Dundonald, *My Army Life* (London, 1926), 191.
[45]*Ibid*, 262.
[46]Canada, *House of Commons Debates*, LXVI (1904), 5498.

Hutton wrote to Minto from Australia: "Dundonald has been experiencing the same logrolling and parti-political immoralities to which I was subjected . . . It seems as if he had then allowed himself to lose his temper and publicly impugn the Government he was serving. If so, he, poor fellow, has put himself entirely in the wrong".[47]

This was precisely the view of the Governor-General, and when Dundonald called at Government House on June 11 Minto did not disguise his disapproval. "I told him he must clearly understand that I could not possibly approve of the line of action he had adopted . . . I also told him that I felt sure exceptions would be taken to the assistance he had sought from Col. Sam Hughes as an opposition member".[48]

To Laurier he made no attempt to defend the G.O.C. but Fisher, he thought, should resign from the cabinet. Instead the cabinet exonerated Fisher in an Order-in-Council rescinding the appointment of Dundonald. Minto signed the Order, brought to him by Dr. Borden, but at midnight sent a note to Laurier suggesting that the wording might be changed from a dismissal to a request for recall. When no change was made, the Governor-General, through his secretary, sent a message to council strongly censuring Fisher's interference in the militia as "entirely subversive of constitutional government".[49]

Laurier called upon Minto with a copy of the memorandum in his hand. "This is a very weighty document, Your Excellency," he said. "Do you intend to dismiss your ministers?" Minto affirmed that he had no such intention, that the memorandum was not to be placed in the Archives or tabled on request of the opposition. The interview ended on a constitutional note. "So long," said Minto "as I retained the services of my ministers I should not be justified in adopting a line which would place me before the public as censuring their action. I felt that if I did so I should step down into the political arena and should at once myself become a centre around which the political storm would rage."[50]

On a division of the House over Dundonald's dismissal, the Government was sustained by a vote of 84 to 42. The Earl "very sore at the manner of his dismissal" went to see Minto in a truculent frame of mind and "used very strong language as regards Borden and especially as to Sir Wilfrid Laurier whom he said he hated and wished to do him all the harm he could".[51] Minto, the same day, wrote to Laurier commending the remarks he had made in the House about Dundonald's military career, observing once more that political pressure was ruinous to any military force and concluding, with relief, "I am so glad to think the matter is over for the present, and hope to be off to Cascapedia on Monday night . . . I hear salmon are very scarce".[52]

[47]Minto Papers, Hutton to Minto, 21 June, 1904.
[48]Ibid, Minto to Lyttleton, 11 June, 1904.
[49]Ibid, Memorandum to Council, 15 June, 1904.
[50]Ibid, Minto to Lyttleton, 17 June, 1904.
[51]Ibid, 25 June, 1904.
[52]Laurier Papers, Minto to Laurier, 25 June, 1904.

To return to Dafoe's strictures upon Lord Minto, there is little if anything in the Minto or Laurier Papers to substantiate the charges, nothing that even faintly suggests the blunt country squire or the blustering heavy dragoon. Each at times called the other "stiff"; there were honest differences of opinion, but instead of continuous struggle there was a friendly approach to all problems and a deepening respect for each other. To an unusual degree they shared their fears, their confidences, and their triumphs. In a letter thanking the Governor-General for a farewell gift, Laurier sums up their relations:

". . . I regard this parting gift as an additional evidence of what you have often told me, *viz.* that the relations which have existed between Your Excellency as representative of the King and myself as first servant of the Crown in this country have been satisfactory to you. They certainly have been most satisfactory to me. As I look back upon these last six years, I feel happy and proud that there never occurred between us any disagreement and even very few differences of opinion . . . Allow me the pleasure of conveying to you and to Lady Minto the grateful and heartfelt good wishes of a very true friend . . ."[53]

[53]Minto Papers, Laurier to Minto, Nov. 1904.

Sir Wilfrid Laurier and the British
Preferential Tariff System

JAMES A. COLVIN

WHEN IN April, 1897, the Laurier Government announced its intention to give a tariff preference to goods imported into Canada from the United Kingdom, the London *Times* recorded that "Conservatives and Liberals alike have hardly yet recovered from the astonishment with which the new tariff has affected them." [1] Astonishment was certainly the word for it, for the new tariff was completely at odds with the commercial policy which the Liberals had been advocating zealously throughout the previous decade. In the years preceding their sudden reversal of 1897 Liberal spokesmen had called for intimacy with the United States in terms of commercial union or unrestricted reciprocity; and it was in fact but six years earlier that the party had met political defeat in pursuit of that very course.

For their pains the Liberals thus paid dearly. Imperial sentiment was a formidable factor in political affairs at the time and Canadians of the day regarded intimacy with the United States as the very antithesis of that with the United Kingdom. These facts Sir John Macdonald knew and exploited. Affirming his determination to die a British subject, Macdonald burdened the Liberals with the charge of disloyalty sufficiently to win the election of 1891 and to impress upon his opponents the need for a modified policy. Modification of Liberal opinion came slowly, but come it did; and in subsequent years steps were taken to accommodate and win support from those electors who had hitherto favoured the British leanings of the Conservatives. Eventually came the unheralded British Preference and in part on that account a Liberal heyday. Then in 1911 the opportunity for reciprocity with the United States again prevailed, and the Liberals prepared to return to their first love. But again the Canadian electorate intervened and as in 1891 the Liberals went down to defeat.

Thus between their two unsuccessful campaigns for reciprocity with the United States, the Liberals in 1897 sandwiched a tariff preference for the United Kingdom; and with Joseph Chamberlain at the Colonial Office to give their venture the support it appeared to solocit, they inadvertently inaugurated a new era in the history of imperial commerce.

Before he became leader of the Liberal Party in 1887 Wilfred Laurier had gone on record at one stage or another in favour of both protection and free trade, but he had never actually figured prominently in the trade question, and this perhaps accounts for the fact that he has since been regarded by some students as a free trader and by others as a protectionist. But whatever his attitude toward the basic principles, following his election as Liberal leader, he swung rapidly in favour of "some kind of reciprocity with the United States." [2] He

---

[1] *The Times*, April 24, 1897. For a more detailed analysis of Laurier's trade policies, see the author's unpublished Ph.D. thesis, *Sir Wilfrid Laurier and the Imperial Problem, 1896-1906,* Unversity of London, 1954.

[2] Sir Wilfrid Laurier Papers, Public Archives of Canada, undated letters to members of the Liberal Party, 1887.

Reprinted from Canadian Historical Association, *Report,* 1955

was not yet prepared to say so publicly, but to his colleagues he wrote stressing that while "the idea is still uncertain", commercial union "is the most advantageous that the people of Canada could look to." [3] The crucial question, however, was "whether if commercial union is to be made an article of our programme it would be advisable to do so at once, or to wait for some future occasion." [4]

Before a year had passed the party leaders had made up their minds. The policy of unrestricted reciprocity with the United States was adopted at a party caucus on March 14, 1888, and from this time on Laurier, Cartwright, and John Charlton were particularly active in educating the country to its virtues. [5] In 1891 Laurier fought his first election as Liberal leader on a platform of unrestricted reciprocity. But his effort was unsuccessful, and because of the annexationist implications associated with the proposition prominent Liberals were now writing to him "suggesting that the party quietly drop its policy." [6] Still Laurier pressed on, though in doing so he appears to have been one of the more insistent of a small minority.

Following the elections of 1891 Laurier made two trips to the United States to discuss trade relations. In a speech at Boston in November he outlined his aims which he based upon the possible separation of Canada from the Mother Country. "The first article in the programme of the Liberal party", he said,

> is to establish absolute reciprocal freedom of trade between Canada and the United States for all the products of the two countries whether natural or manufactured. Our object is . . . to offer to the United States the free entrance to our territory of all American products, provided the United States extend the same privileges to the products of Canada. [7]

At the same time Laurier took the opportunity of discounting the proposal for "an Imperial Trade League whereby England and her possessions would be united to trade together to the exclusion of the rest of the world."

Clearly then, Laurier's objectives had not changed since the March elections, notwithstanding the unhappy results. But the Liberals were not insensible to the political force of the country's imperial sentiment, and at their convention in Ottawa in 1893 they suggested that the benefits of reciprocity with the United States would be confined not merely to Canada but "that the interests alike of the Dominion and the Empire would be materially advanced by the establishment of such relations." [8]

Meanwhile John Charlton was posted to Washington "to watch proceedings in reference to the tariff changes" and to keep tab on what

[3] *Ibid.*

[4] *Ibid.* This point was also raised in another letter dated July 14th.

[5] Sir John Willison, *Sir Wilfrid Laurier*, The Makers of Canada, (Toronto, 1926), IX, ii, 147-50.

[6] See Underhill, F. H., "Laurier and Blake, 1882-1891", *Canadian Historical Review*, December, 1939, 403-4.

[7] *The Globe*, November 27, 1891, p. 5.

[8] *Official Report of the Liberal Convention*, 1893, Ottawa, p. 81.

the Conservatives were doing. [9]   In Parliament the latter were the subject of a full-scale attack for their failure to establish reciprocity, which
in the main their opponents attributed to the Government's protective
instincts and false sense of loyalty.   On the last point Laurier made it
clear that he himself suffered no inhibitions.   "I am ready any day,"
he said, "whether I am charged with annexation or not, to take a
Yankee dollar in preference to an English shilling;" [10] while to a
Boston audience he declared his willingness, if the need arose, to be
hostile to Britain. [11]

So inclined, the Liberals prepared for the 1896 elections by
issuing a pamphlet in which they stressed the importance of free trade,
reeciprocity, and the United States; [12] and two months before the elections Edward Farrer was able to inform a United States Tariff Commission that the Liberals' reciprocity plank of 1893 was still "their
platform today". [13]

Events were about at this stage when the Conservatives under
Tupper began to reassert the virtues of imperial preference, and the
Liberals showed concern. [14]   John Willison advised Laurier to soft-
pedal reciprocity; [15] while Mowat wrote, urging him before it was too
late to make a public statement on tariff which would appeal to
wavering Conservatives. [16]   Laurier heeded counsel and changed his
tack to catch some of the prevailing breeze.   In a speech at London,
Ontario, he reviewed the question in a way which suggested that the
Liberals far more than the Conservatives had their minds on imperial
preference, and *The Globe* spread the good word throughout Ontario
the next day. [17]

Shortly after the elections, however, the party's thoughts turned
again to reciprocity.   In September, Cartwright, in Washington to
discuss issues arising out of the Venezuela boundary dispute, sounded
Joseph Chamberlain on the possibility of Canada throwing in her
commercial lot with the United States; [18] while shortly afterwards
Laurier was looking for a favourable opportunity to go to Washington
himself. The Republic was just then settling down after a presidential
election, however, and John Charlton advised the Prime Minister to
bide his time. [19]   Accordingly, Laurier waited, but he entrusted the
task to Charlton and Edward Farrer; and subsequently he, Cartwright,

[9] Curnoe, L. J., *John Charlton and Canadian-American Relations,* unpublished
M.A. thesis, University of Toronto, 1939, p. 88.
[10] Canada, Parliament, House of Commons, *Debates,* 1892, I, 1144.
[11] See *ibid.,* 1894, I, 1859.
[12] See *Platform of the Liberal Party of Canada,* 1895, pp. 11, 55, 61-3. Also
see *Federal Elections,* 1895, *the Issues of the Campaign,* pp. 21, 58-62.
[13] April 16, 1896. See United States Congress. H. R. *Report of the Committee
on Ways and Means concerning Reciprocity and Commercial Treaties,* 1896, p. 69.
[14] See Sir Charles Tupper, *Recollections of Sixty Years in Canada,* (Toronto,
1914), p. 254.
[15] Sir John Willison, *Reminiscences, Political and Personal,* (Toronto, 1919),
p. 296.
[16] Laurier Papers, May 22, 1896.
[17] *The Globe,* June 4, 1896, p. 4.
[18] J. L. Garvin, *The Life of Joseph Chamberlain,* (3 v., London, 1932-1934),
III, 184.
[19] See Laurier Papers, Charlton to Laurier, December 15, 1896.

and Sir Louis Davies also paid their respects to the new American administration.

But in all their attempts the Liberals were unsuccessful, and to make matters worse the Dingley Bill was now clearly on the horizon and their own budget day forthcoming. Although Laurier had Farrer at Washington to advise him of any change on the part of the Republicans, the Liberals were becoming convinced "that no proposals looking towards a . . . reciprocity treaty . . . would be entertained", [20] and they began to ponder a change of strategy. As the Americans had no ear for the suppliant, the Liberals elected to take a firmer stand and on the off chance that the Republicans might be susceptible to their own tactics, they prepared to give tit for tat.

"I am strongly impressed with the view that our relations with our neighbours should be friendly," Laurier wrote to Charlton, "at the same time I am equally strong in the opinion that we may have to take the American tariff . . . and make it the Canadian Tariff." [21]

Macdonald had suggested reprisal as the key to reciprocity two decades earlier, [22] and it was precisely in this direction that the Liberals were now inclining. The party leaders were well aware that sections 3 and 4 of the Dingley Bill, confining though they were, still offered a degree of scope for reciprocity; though whether or not the Republicans would agree to negotiate even within these limits was of course another thing. [23] In any event it was under just such ominous circumstances that William Fielding rose in the House of Commons on April 22 to deliver the budget and amend the tariff. To the despair of the party's free traders, the proposed tariff was much like that of the Conservatives. It was to remain protective and to retain the standing offer of reciprocity written into it by the Conservatives in 1879. [24] But here the similarity ended, for the Conservative offer of reciprocity had been directed simply toward the United States. The Liberals now made it to "all the world." More extenuating than the offer itself, however, was the interpretation placed upon it. Singularly qualified for the preference inherent in the new tariff clause, said Fielding, was not the United States, but the United Kingdom.

The implied departure from the party's traditional policy was more apparent than real. In his budget speech Fielding admitted that a treaty with the United States was still the party's intent. [25] But until the Americans were prepared to negotiate the best that the Liberals could do was adjust the tariff Act in a way that would render it readily adaptable to any change on the part of the Republicans. This the offer of reciprocal preference did to perfection, since the qualification for the preference was simply reciprocal treatment. At the same time, by conferring the preference upon Great Britain while applying the general tariff to the United States, the Canadian Govern-

20 See J. M. V. Foster, "Reciprocity and the Joint High Commission of 1898-1899," *Report of the Canadian Historical Association,* 1939, p. 88.
21 Laurier Papers, January 18, 1897. .
22 Canada, Parliament, House of Commons, *Debates,* 1878, p. 862.
23 See *United States Statutes at Large,* 1897-9, v. 30, Sec. 3, 4.
24 Statutes of Canada, 1879, 42 Victoria, C. 15, Sec. 6.
25 Canada, Parliament, House of Commons, *Debates,* 1897, I, 1134, 1254-5.

ment was actually exerting pressure on the Americans to comply with
the terms of its latest offer.

In the comedy of errors which now was about to transpire the
Mother Country was thus intended to play a major role. She was
selected by the government of her senior dominion as the trade correspondent necessary to allow its new tariff scheme to function, since by
the very terms of the tariff there had to be some one with whom to
reciprocate; she was used to impress upon the Americans should they
remain obdurate that Canada could project her trade in other directions; and more extenuating than either of these, her nomination by
the Canadian Government as the recipient of the preference was a
titbit to satisfy the Dominion's imperial sentiment and demands for a
pro-British tariff. [26]

Doubtful of the American market, the Liberal board of strategy
simply deduced that Great Britain by her unique policy of free trade
had met the prescribed terms of the new tariff and thereupon made her
the recipient of the preference. [27] The illogical conclusion that the
Mother Country was so entitled was of course frought with dangerous
implications on account of Great Britain's numerous agreements with
other countries. But this the Liberals elected to ride over roughshod.
England neither sought nor qualified for the dubious advantage
imposed upon her and Canada acquired no advantage in return. Her
products entered the United Kingdom as before — in open competition
and on the basis of free trade.

In spite of such anomalies the concession to the Mother Country
ascribed to the Fielding tariff a quasi-imperialist air not easily discoun-
tenanced; for the renascent imperialism of the time, along with the
emphasis which was sometimes ignorantly and sometimes wilfully
placed upon the British advantage implied in the tariff, denied the facts.
By their unilateral action in making a free and unsolicited grant to
the Mother Country, the Canadian Liberals appeared to have taken a
deliberate step toward the founding of a new imperial economic order.
But meanwhile from behind the scenes at Washington, a despairing
Charlton wrote to Laurier,

> I have decided to take pretty high ground before the Subcommittee tonight
> for if the policy that has been entered upon at Washington is continued, we
> may just as well tell the Yankee to go to Hades and we will go to England. [28]

Two months after the introduction of the Fielding tariff Laurier
was in London to attend the first of Joseph Chamberlain's Colonial
Conferences. To all but the most cynical, both in Canada and
England, the tariff and the conference appeared to be expressions of
a common purpose. Laurier was the hero of the hour. But as the
Conference approached the Canadian Premier saw that the preferential
tariff might serve another purpose. For some years the Liberals had
sought to free Canada from the all-embracing commercial treaties
which the United Kingdom had negotiated with foreign countries on

---

[26] See Laurier Papers, Willison to Laurier, April 12, 1897.
[27] Canada, Parliament, House of Commons, *Debates*, 1897, I, 2985.
[28] Laurier Papers, April 30, 1897.

behalf of the Empire at large.   As a step toward Canadian commercial
freedom Blake had called for the denunciation of such treaties in
1882 [29] with Laurier and Cartwright supporting him, and Laurier had
since done so repeatedly. [30]

The essential feature of these "most favoured nation" or "parity
of treatment" treaties was a clause precluding preferential tariff treatment for any third country on the part of either of the contracting
parties.   But even more crippling were the clauses written into Great
Britain's agreements with Belgium (1862) and Germany (1865)
which actually went the length of preventing differential treatment by
British colonies on behalf of the Mother Country; and it was by virtue
of this fact that George E. Foster's proposals for intra-imperial trade
had foundered at the Ottawa Conference of 1894. [31]

The recent grant of preference to the Mother Country was in
violation of the Belgian and German treaties, but from London the
Canadian Premier had already received word that the time for contest-
ing them was opportune.   Sir Howard Vincent, the secretary of the
United Empire Trade League, had written enthusiastically to assure
him

> that if Germany and Belgium set up their treaties . . . against your pro-
> posals, no pains shall be spared to bring about their immediate denun-
> ciation. [32]

So primed, and conscious of Chamberlain's determination to effect
imperial unity whatever the means, Laurier attended the Conference as
the sponsor of imperial commercial unity, to which he represented the
Belgian and German treaties as impediments.   Impressed with Laurier's
stand and the suggestion that he was encouraging the other colonial
premiers to follow Canada's lead, Chamberlain took up the cause.   At
the conclusion of the conference Belgium and Germany were informed
that Her Majesty's Government desired to terminate the commercial
treaties to which they were party at the end of July, 1898: after which
date all British colonies would be free to give a tariff preference to the
Mother Country, should they so desire.

Regarding the United States and other countries, however, the
Canadian preferential tariff system was still not out of the woods, for
the Law Officers of the Crown after studying the question and hearing
the Canadian point of view, decreed that whatever befell the Belgian
and German treaties, so long as there existed valid, most favoured
nation, treaties, the Dominion could not grant an independent preference to any third country.   This ruling had the two-fold effect of
precluding the United States from any immediate preference and
conversely of limiting the Canadian preference to Great Britain and
her possessions.   And in the final analysis it left the Canadian Government with no alternative but to do the latter or rescind the Fielding
tariff altogether.

[29] Canada, Parliament, House of Commons, *Debates*, 1882, p. 1075.
[30] *Ibid.*, 1889, I, 172-93; 1891, III, 6351; 1892, I, 1143.
[31] *Report of the Colonial Conference*, 1894, C. 7553, p. 5.
[32] Laurier Papers, April 28, 1897.

Advised of the Law Officers' decision while he was still in England, Laurier informed Chamberlain that under the circumstances Canada would alter its tariff "so as to confine its operation to the United Kingdom and British possessions." [33] This decision was aligned with the Mother Country's termination of the Belgian and German treaties; and on August 1, 1898, the very day that termination took effect the Canadian preferential tariff entered the second stage of its metamorphosis. On August 1, 1898, the Canadian tariff changed from *reciprocal* to *British* preference.

To outward appearances Laurier and Chamberlain were working hand in glove. But from Ottawa, Cartwright, Charlton and Davies continued to visit Washington, and shortly after his return from the Conference Laurier was himself at the American capital to see what could be done about reciprocity. During the next two years the visits continued, and Cartwright, Charlton and Davies were nominated as Canadian representatives on the reciprocity committee of the Joint High Commission which met during the winter of 1898-9.

It was about this time that Canadian public opinion showed a renewed hardening against proposals for reciprocity with the United States, a point on which Laurier received all too frequent reminders from his colleagues in Canada. Disgruntled but not dissuaded, he wrote to John Willison from Washington:

> If anything could discourage me it would be the attitude now maintained by our friends in Ontario, who instead of supporting us are preparing the ground for the attacks of the Tories against us . . . . We have held up the idea . . . that we should have more friendly relations with our neighbours and now that we are engaged in the task our friends urge us not to go any further . . . . There is a feeling . . . that I could make myself a hero by . . . breaking off . . . negotiations . . . and coming back to Canada . . . . But when a commercial warfare would be raging . . . what then . . . ? I think on this occasion again I shall act on my own judgment . . . and I will depend on you to defend me. [34]

Once again the Canadian delegation made little headway against the American protectionists, and at the conclusion of the meetings Laurier declared to Willison that he would "never again . . . meet our American friends in conference until I should have in advance, and in writing, a certainty of the concessions which we should make." [35] But in the autumn the Prime Minister again found occasion to travel south of the border and he took advantage of the opportunity to tell members of the Chicago Board of Trade that if his efforts to extend Canadian-American trade relations succeeded it would mark the crowning success of his life. [36]

It was during his absence from Canada on this occasion that the South African War began. Involved in spite of itself, the government saw fit to increase the incidence of the British tariff preference from twenty-five to thirty-three and one-third per cent; and in the subsequent Speech from the Throne Canadian participation in the war

[33] C.O. 42, 850, July 15, 1897.
[34] Sir John Willison Papers, Public Archives of Canada, January 7, 1899.
[35] *Ibid.*, February 23, 1899.
[36] See *The Globe*, October 11, 1897.

and the increased preference were carefully reviewed as evidence of the Government's staunch imperial sentiment.

Meanwhile the preference remained unilateral although Conservative critics complained that it should have been mutual; not only to win advantages for Canada over foreign competition in the British market, but also to make the project more unifying. This proposal the Liberals had easily countered with the argument that the divergent trade policies of the two countries rendered such an undertaking impractical. So it was that, much as he would have liked to have obtained a preference for Canada in the markets of the United Kingdom, Laurier had declared after the Conference of 1897 that there was no likelihood of its being accomplished. [37] Having renounced their former allegiance to free trade for practical purposes, the Liberals were thus on solid ground; and there seemed every reason to believe as Fielding had asserted that there was no probability "in the immediate or early future" of the British people adopting preferential trade on the basis of protection. [38]

Then the bombshell burst. To help defray the costs of the war in South Africa Sir Michael Hicks Beach reimposed the old registration duty on corn imported into Great Britain and in doing so he cut deeply into Laurier's argument for a unilateral preference. Rumours that the Mother Country might put a tax on foodstuffs had reached Canada toward the end of 1901, and had immediately evoked from a number of municipal Boards of Trade demands that in such an event the Dominion Government should take steps to secure preferential treatment for Canadian produce. In the weeks that followed the Prime Minister's office was deluged with letters of a similar tone. Members of the Liberal Party spoke for prefference. Commercial bodies and imperialists did likewise; while on the other hand no formidable group appeared to oppose it. The mood of the other self-governing colonies was reputed to be similar to that of Canada, and Sir Charles Tupper declared that under the circumstances "it only remained for Sir Wilfrid Laurier to press the matter to an issue." [39]

The day after Beech's budget speech Robert Borden asked where the Government stood with regard to the new tax. Fielding answered that the Government was still intent on preference but was at the same time reluctant to force the hand of the Mother Counry; and he suggested that a tax which was nothing less than a consequence of the war in South Africa should not be looked upon in the same light as if it had been imposed in time of peace. [40] Meanwhile Laurier cabled Lord Strathcona to ascertain the feelings of Beech and Chamberlain regarding preferential treatment for Canadian wheat and flour. [41] But while the new duties were drawing the fire of doubting free traders in England, government policy in Canada remained vague and ill-defined. Laurier's replies to Borden's questions drew from one of the latter's followers the caustic complaint that

37 *Ibid.*, October 7, 1897
38 Canada, Parliament, House of Commons, *Debates*, 1898, I, 3139.
39 See *Canadian Annual Review*, 1902, 133.
40 See Canada, Parliament, House of Commons, *Debates*, 1902, I, 2739-53.
41 Laurier Papers, April 15, 1902.

We have listened as usual with delight to the eloquent words of the leader of the Government and I defy any honourable gentleman to stand . . . and say what is the policy that the Government intend to carry out when they go to England. [42]

Meanwhile Laurier's problem was being partially solved by the assurances emanating from the British Government that the corn tax was entirely disassociated from either imperial trade or protection. Accordingly, when eventually Borden drove Laurier to say that he would seek a preference for Canadian wheat, the fat, in London, was in the fire.

Referring to the Canadian debate, Campbell-Bannerman asked the Government at Westminster whether the duties were the foundation of a new imperial policy. [43] Although Balfour assured the House to the contrary the Opposition remained doubtful. They argued that the principle of protection was inherent in the tax, and that consequently Canada could no longer be assuaged with the claim that Great Britain's fiscal policy precluded preferential treatment for the colonies. So events progressed until mid-June when Hicks Beech disclaimed altogether any association between the new tax, the colonies, or Sir Wilfrid Laurier's attendance at the pending Colonial Conference. [44]

Beech's speech enabled Laurier to press for preference without running the risk of obtaining it, and he arrived in England to receive from his Secretary of State, Sir Richard Scott, a quasi-congratulatory reference to the speech.

Beech has made your line of action re preferential trade easy. He seems to have given Chamberlain the snub. I always felt that the latter could not carry his views . . . so that question has its quietus, though *The Mail* still harps on it and hopes you will put Sir M. H. Beech right. [45]

The Canadian Premier had arrived in London about the middle of June, and immediately applied himself to a study of the trade question. He discussed it both with members of the Government and of the Liberal Opposition, [46] and he knew how intense was the feeling against protection and especially against the use of the corn duties as a medium of preferential treatment for the colonies. [47] Colonel G. T. Denison who had just completed a lecture tour of the Mother Country urging the adoption of mutual preference has recorded that,

When Sir Wilfrid Laurier came over just before the Conference, knowing that I had been discussing the subject for two months, he asked me if I thought the proposition I had been advocating could be proposed at the Conference with any prospect of success. I replied that I did not think it could, that Great Britain was not ready for it, that Australia at the time was engaged in such a struggle over her revenue tariff that she could not act, and that if I was in his place I should not attempt it. [48]

[42] Canada, Parliament, House of Commons, *Debates*, 1902, II, 4732.
[43] *British Parliamentary Debates, House of Commons*, 1902, VIII, 151-4.
[44] See *ibid.*, IX, 167.
[45] Laurier Papers, June 26, 1902.
[46] See Viscount Simon, *Retrospect, The Memoirs of the Rt. Hon. Viscount Simon*, (London, 1952). pp. 66-7; Hewins, W. A. S., *The Apologia of an Imperialist*, (2 v., London, 1929), I, 119.
[47] See *ibid.*
[48] Colonel G. T. Denison, *The Struggle for Imperial Unity*, (London and Toronto, 1909), p. 341.

The Conference proper began on June 30 and was just nicely started, when the King underwent an appendectomy and Chamberlain suffered a cab accident. It was thus not until July the 18th that commercial relations were discussed. In the meantime Laurier, who had been joined by four members of his Cabinet, continued to take soundings; and when the Conference resumed the Canadian Premier, reversing his stand of 1897, pressed strongly for a colonial preference in the markets of the Mother Country.

The request of the Canadian Ministers . . . for reciprocal preference marked, therefore, a distinct change in the policy of the Liberal Party with reference to the preferential duty. [49]

Chamberlain was now in a difficult position. His hopes for imperial military and political unity had already suffered setbacks, and commerce seemed the only way. But from the Canadians came threats that unless reciprocation for the preference already accorded the Mother Country was soon forthcoming, the Canadian grant might be repealed; from the free traders of England came opposition to any proposal entailing in particular a tax on food. And when in 1903 C. T. Ritchie prevailed upon the British Cabinet to repeal the corn duties rather than grant Canada a preference, Chamberlain had lost his medium of exchange.

For the Colonial Secretary the situation was now worse than before. His imperial policy was in direct conflict with his country's fiscal policy, and to meet the Canadian demands he would now have to establish duties on which to base a preference for the Dominion. This was out and out protectionism, and Chamberlain knew it. Rather than abandon the fruits of his labours at the Colonial Office, however, he determined to make the try. In September, 1903, he resigned from the Cabinet and shortly after he launched his campaign for tariff reform.

Chamberlain's decision to resign and campaign for tariff reform was made on the understanding that he would have the co-operation of the Canadian ministers in establishing a comprehensive system of mutual preferences. But it is now apparent that the Canadian ultimatum which prompted his action was served not so much to win preference from the United Kingdom as to provide an escape from further entanglement in the system of imperial commerce which they themselves had accidently inaugurated in 1897. Instead of co-operating as Chamberlain expected them to, the Canadian ministers stood aloof from the tariff reform movement, once it was underway.

In 1905 Chamberlain actually sent a representative to consult with Laurier and Fielding with a view to presenting the British electorate with an outline of what additional preferential treatment the Dominion would give the Mother Country in return for any preference accorded Canada. But Laurier and Fielding were non-committal. They proffered no proposals, except to repeat that they might withdraw the original preference; and they were specific on but one point — there must be a preference for Canadian wheat.

[49] *Colonial Tariff Policies.* Report of the United States Tariff Commission of 1922, p. 671.

Under the circumstances Chamberlain prepared to walk the last mile alone. He had reached no understanding with the Canadians as Taft was able to do in 1911. He had no attractive alternatives to put before his country men; and he had, in fact, to admit that the adoption of mutual preference would entail a duty on grain. The British elections on January 12 and 13, 1906, resulted in the most crushing defeat of the Conservative Party since the days of the first Reform Bill. The dangerous implications of imperial integration inherent in the preferential scheme had been removed by the votes of the British electors, and the Canadian Government could now back out of the system, at leisure. Under the circumstances Laurier and Fielding regained the grace and composure that had been theirs in 1897.

Three weeks after the elections, Laurier wrote to the secretary of Chamberlain's Tariff Reform League. "We are now . . . preparing . . . our tariff. I may tell you, as indeed you probably know, that we have no intention of discontinuing the British preference."[50] In November, Fielding presented his eleventh budget. Since the elections in the United Kingdom he too felt more kindly toward the Mother Country. "We adhere to the principle of British preference," he said, "because . . . we believe it has been a good thing for Canada . . . . It has given Canada prominence in the eyes of the empire and all over the world." [51]

In England the free trading Liberals had come into power to bang, bolt, and bar the door against the principle of tariffs for imperial preference; and in Canada the Liberals, exonerated by their own superficial request for preference and the action of the British voters, were free to cast about in other directions for preferred trade correspondents. As far as the Laurier Government was concerned, British preference had run its course. The original purpose of the project had not been realized, for the American market still lay behind a protective wall. But Canada had been liberated from two of the more confining of Britain's imperial commercial treaties, and pro-British votes had been won into the bargain. The way to Washington was still not open, of course, but if and when it should be, the Government was excellently placed to say that it had done its best for imperial trade, and that the rejection of the plan was of British doing.

[50] Laurier Papers, Laurier to W. A. S. Hewins, February 7, 1906.
[51] Canada, Parliament, House of Commons, *Debates*, 1906-7, I, 289-90.

General Hutton and the Problem of Military Imperialism in Canada, 1898-1900

NORMAN PENLINGTON

THE eighteen-nineties were a period of crucial change in international relations. They were years marked by the world-wide building and consolidation of empires in defence of threatened economic interests, the threats arising basically from the fact that markets were narrowing at the very time when the productive capacity of all nations demanded larger fields of economic exploitation, even at the price of war. Consequently the nations rushed into a gigantic armament race to protect their only sure markets —colonies. Britain with the largest empire was severely exposed and felt most seriously the need of strengthening the defences of her empire. As part of her efforts the British government despatched General Hutton to improve the defences of Canada. Even though Canada was one of the least threatened and one of the least militaristic countries of the world, Hutton carried out his mission with the greatest vigour. While, therefore, his régime in Canada is in a sense of small importance, nevertheless it illustrates in an illuminating way certain important aspects of Canada's relations with Britain, and it marks an increasing participation by Canada in imperial affairs, which gradually grew into world affairs.

I

Canada in 1898 paid the lowest per capita military tax in the world—thirty-three cents per head. That fact reveals more eloquently than any description the indifference of Canadians to problems of defence. Three reasons account for their unconcern. First, in the prosperous years at the turn of the century the economic development of Canada monopolized the full attention of Canadians. Secondly, the French Canadians, although wholeheartedly subscribing to the needs of the economic development of Canada as they understood it, were not conscious of interests lying beyond their own borders, and especially of any necessity for fighting on alien soil. Thirdly, Canada, "as daughter in her mother's house," nestling safely behind the bulwark of the British navy and the bastion of the Monroe Doctrine, saw little need of shouldering a big burden of defence.[1] Each British officer commanding the Canadian Militia added a fourth reason—politics.

[1]Cf. Laurier's statement to the Earl of Dundonald, the last General Officer Commanding: "You must not take the Militia seriously . . . as the Monroe Doctrine protects against enemy aggression" (Earl of Dundonald, *My Army Life*, London, 1926, 191).

Reprinted from *Canadian Historical Review*, XXIV (2), June, 1943

Politics, he complained, was the cancer eating into the whole
defence system. But the cancer was a result rather than a cause;
it grew from the complete apathy of Canadians to military affairs.
Until stirring and frightening events should jolt Canadian public
opinion out of its complacency, mock militarism would plague
Canada's defences.

The Venezuela crisis first tore away the veil of indifference to
reveal a picture that could only inspire anxiety for Canada's
safety. This newly awakened fear provided the public support
for the two outstanding reforms undertaken in 1896 and 1897 by
the new Liberal Minister of Militia, Dr. F. W. Borden. He increased the number of militiamen trained in camp from 10,462 to
35,035 and limited the tenure of command to five years. Nothing
shows better the downright senility and deadness of the Canadian
Militia than the fact that of ninety-two battalion commanders
thirty-seven averaged eighteen years' continuous command![2]

A more important influence in improving the defences was
the efforts of Joseph Chamberlain, the leader in Britain of the
movement for imperial consolidation. On becoming Colonial
Secretary in 1895 he began to rally the forces of the British Empire
by all possible means. In conjunction with the War Office,
Chamberlain exerted uninterrupted pressure on the colonies to
augment land and naval forces and to improve their efficiency.
One of the best opportunities for discussing imperial defence came
at the Colonial Conference of 1897. Although Chamberlain failed
to gain definite military commitments, he secured the formal
acceptance of the principle of uniformity in organization, training,
and equipment, and an agreement to establish closer co-operation
among the Defence Departments of the empire.[3] At that Conference too, Dr. Borden invited the British government to despatch
a committee to examine the state of Canada's defences and to
propose a plan for their improvement. Though the Canadian
government accepted the comprehensive report of the committee,
it did not put all its recommendations into effect.[4]

The resignations in 1898 of the Governor-General and the
General Officer Commanding paved the way for the appointment
of two outstanding and vigorous imperialists—Lord Minto and
Major-General E. T. H. Hutton. From the point of view of the

[2]I am gratefully indebted for this information to memoranda written by Lieutenant-
Colonel F. Cummins of the Historical Section of the Canadian General Staff, Ottawa,
and culled from militia files. It is to be noted, however, that Dr. Borden put into
operation his predecessor's plan of increasing the number of militiamen in camp.
    [3]*Ibid.*   [4]*Ibid.*

British authorities no man could better fill the post of governor-general than Lord Minto, since he possessed a wide knowledge of Canadian military conditions gained as military secretary to Lord Lansdowne, 1883-5. In those years he filled the positions of chief of staff in the Rebellion of 1885 and of organizer of the voyageurs that were despatched to Egypt. The latter experience was invaluable, for it enabled him to find out and to cope with the difficulties of sending Canadian troops overseas, and to become aware of the possibility of Canada's one day officially helping in an empire war.[5] Moreover, since Lord Minto thoroughly understood the steps to be taken to make an efficient Canadian Militia, he worked discreetly, as far as his position would allow, in close collaboration with General Hutton and provided him with stubborn support against the opposition of the Cabinet. But the actual mission of reforming the Militia and of creating a favourable public opinion for its activities—that was the task of the new General Officer Commanding.

II

Major-General E. T. H. Hutton was a brilliant and energetic soldier with advanced military ideas, and was one of the leading military disciples of Lord Wolseley, the British Commander-in-Chief. Backed by the knowledge that he was a personal aide-de-camp to the Queen, having the full support of the Governors and the Colonial Secretary, Hutton unsparingly criticized the armies of the colonies, demanded implicit obedience from his soldiers, and attempted to dictate to local governments.

These tactics he pursued each time he held the position of General Officer Commanding—in New South Wales (1893-6), in Canada (1898-1900), and in the Commonwealth of Australia (1901-4). Partly because of Australia's isolation and of her consequent need for adequate defence, the prestige of the soldier ranked higher than in Canada; hence Hutton had a freer hand unconstitutionally to bend governments to his will and ruthlessly to reform the militias. For example, he frequently boasted that he had driven the Dibbs government in New South Wales from office.[6] Later, when he was General Officer Commanding in the

[5]*Vide* the invaluable letter of Lord Melgund (later Lord Minto) to Goldwin Smith, March 1, 1885 (Arnold Haultain, ed., *Goldwin Smith's Correspondence*, Toronto, 1913, 167).

[6]Sir George Dibbs told Sir Mackenzie Bowell that he had resigned because of his unauthorized use of troops to quell rioters in a strike (*Canada, Debates of the Senate*, March 20, 1900, 208).

Commonwealth, Sir William Lyne, the Minister of Defence, had to resort to strong measures against him "in connection with the establishment of a school of instruction." Sir William explained to the House that since the General persisted in proceeding contrary to instructions, he "had to stop supplies in order to compel submission to the authority in control of the finances."[7] In Canada too, Hutton trod an unconstitutional path, but without open opposition to the civil power.

Although in Hutton's case an arrogant personality undoubtedly played a big part in the disputes, yet the very nature of the office of General Officer Commanding created difficulty, and if the incumbent were energetic and imperialistic, it produced explosion. To avoid trouble the General had to bear in mind four points of friction. First, public apathy with regard to military matters would lead a general in his enthusiasm for military improvement to exasperation, and any show of feeling or disdain for colonials, such as Englishmen in those days were often prone to display, simply afforded popular justification for the government's treatment of him. Thus, secondly, both sensitive colonials and budding nationalists found Hutton's irritating manner a convenient excuse for blocking the General. Thirdly, the legal position of the General Officer Commanding was fraught with deceptive ambiguity. The phrase in the Militia Act of 1887—"an officer holding the rank of Colonel . . . in Her Majesty's regular army, who shall be charged under the order of Her Majesty with the military command and discipline of the Militia . . ."[8]—was interpreted by the General Officer Commanding as meaning that he was superior in authority to his employer, the Canadian government, an interpretation which would not be countenanced for a moment.[9] But he failed to see how two other sections whittled down that apparently broad power; the next section laid down that the Governor in Council should set forth the duties of the General Officer Commanding; and Section 4 of the Act declared that "the Minister of Militia and Defence shall have the initiative in all Militia affairs involving the expenditure of money." Lastly, constitutional conventions did not really exist because of the unimportance of the Militia Department. The Minister of

[7] *Australia, Commonwealth Debates*, Nov. 25, 1904, 1491.
[8] *Revised Statutes of Canada*, 1886, chap. 41, sec. 37.
[9] Public Archives of Canada, Laurier Papers, Correspondence re Hutton, Laurier to Strathcona, Feb. 22, 1900. "It is impossible to understand the conduct of General Hutton except by the assumption that being an officer of the Imperial Army he was superior to the Minister of Militia . . ."

Militia and the General Officer Commanding managed military affairs on a day-to-day basis, and neither hesitated to violate Militia Regulations if it suited the whim of the moment.   One important tendency in departmental policy was that the civil administration arrogated to itself duties that properly belonged to the military.   When General Hutton tried to reclaim those duties he met the implacable opposition of the Minister clinging to what he considered inherent constitutional rights.

Because of the frequency of quarrels between the General Officer Commanding and the Minister over their respective duties, the Generals repeatedly requested the government clearly to define the limits of each one's "powers."   But to these requests the government paid not the slightest attention, preferring a situation, one cannot help feeling, where a misstep might be used as an excuse to dismiss a recalcitrant general.   Furthermore, the government constantly reiterated that since it appointed and paid the General, it had full power to determine his duties.   Only a man possessing a very high degree of tact could fill the position without friction.   But a man of that stamp could not help to prepare opinion nor improve the Canadian Militia in time for war. What was needed in August, 1898, was a man who could practically force reforms on the government; hence, the appointment of Hutton.[10]

In complete contrast to his indolent predecessor, Major-General Hutton immediately on arrival in Canada made a tour of inspection.   His iron will forthwith pulsated through the veins of a wellnigh paralytic militia system.   Critics viewing that unwonted energy with alarm charged that he had come to Canada with a mission; this, he indiscreetly admitted when he revealed that the Secretaries of State for War and the Colonies had given him the following instructions: "Go to Canada and do your utmost to improve their militia, and advise the Government as to the necessary requirements for the defence system," but he hastily added that he alone was responsible for any concrete proposals.[11] In pursuit of that policy he aimed to develop "a military and martial spirit"[12] by delivering speeches at every opportunity.   In these he sketched four themes which were a guide to the public and an indication of his own future plans.

[10]Cf. the appointment in South Africa in the same year of an opposite type of man —Sir William Butler—as Commander-in-Chief.   The Canadians had to be stirred up, the Boers temporarily kept quiet.
[11]Canadian Military Gazette, April 18, 1899, 5.
[12]Ibid., Feb. 21, 1899, 21.

First, to make Canadians glory in their defence forces, he continually referred grandiloquently to the "National Army of Canada" whose object was not only that of protecting Canada but "of participating when necessary in the defence of the Empire."[13] Secondly, to shame Canadians into following his suggestions he unhesitatingly drew attention to the wretched condition of the defence forces. For example, he lectured the people of London, Ontario, on the deplorable state of the local regiment, and then proceeded to make drastic changes in its administrative arrangements.[14] Thirdly, he insisted on the soldiers strictly obeying his commands. Within three weeks of his arrival, he brusquely but characteristically warned his men: "I know my business. I expect you to do your duty; and as a brother officer I shall help you all I can."[15]

Lastly, and most difficult of all, he tried to drive political influence from the Militia and weed out its incompetent officers. Matters, however, were already on the mend even before he arrived, for Dr. Borden had just inaugurated two far-reaching and fundamental reforms—annual camps for all the Militia and limited tenure for officers. Proud of these improvements the Minister naturally chafed at the repeated charges of politics cast at him by the General. The fact was that the word "politics" had different meanings for the two men. To the Minister politics meant discriminating bluntly against the Conservatives. Of course that type of politics everywhere reared its head, but both Borden and Laurier could legitimately complain of what they considered Hutton's blanket accusation of complete partiality for the Liberals. To General Hutton and Lord Minto politics meant the interference of any type of politician in military affairs. No one could deny that.

The resignation of Lieutenant-Colonel Domville gives an instructive example of the problem of politics confronting Hutton.[16] Domville was an incompetent officer who in the previous few years had apparently not even called out his battalion for annual drill.[17] He was already slated for retirement before Hutton came to Canada, but he was a Liberal member of parliament. That explains why Hutton found it so difficult to replace

[13]Toronto *Globe*, March 4, 1899, 19.

[14]*Canadian Military Gazette*, Nov. 1, 1898, 10. The local press later growled that General Hutton thought "we were a lot of half-breeds" (*ibid.*, Dec. 6, 1898, 11).

[15]*Ibid.*, Sept. 6, 1898, 7.

[16]*Canada, Sessional Papers*, 1900, Return 171 . . . for copies of all reports . . . relating to the retirement of Lieutenant-Colonel Domville . . . .

[17]*Canadian Military Gazette*, June 6, 1899, 3.

Domville by Lieutenant-Colonel Markham, who apparently belonged to the Conservative party; why in battling the whole Cabinet to gain his object he himself apparently just escaped being dismissed;[18] why after a whole year's struggle he could only oust Domville by agreeing that Markham should succeed for one week only.[19]

This incident was merely one of the examples of friction that persisted between Hutton and his employers from the beginning. Earlier the government had even refused to confirm his tenure of office and to show him the Report of the Defence Committee of 1898, whose conclusions would have confirmed all Hutton's observations and thus strengthened his own case for improving the Canadian Militia.[20] The reasons for the coolness hardening into hostility varied amongst the members of the Cabinet. All disliked him for conducting himself as an official independent of the Cabinet's authority. R. J. Scott, an Irishman, and Israel Tarte, a French Canadian, also opposed Hutton as the representative of a nation that appeared to them to threaten their races. Dr. Borden, the Minister of Militia, objected not so much to Hutton's policy, in which he tended to take professional pride, but to Hutton's continual pressure. Laurier objected on grounds of high policy. The Prime Minister, knowing full well the point of view of his fellow countrymen, could not acquiesce in the actions of a subordinate official trying to use Canada as a pawn in imperial policy. Undoubtedly too, he must have regarded Hutton's plan of naval defence on Lakes Erie and Ontario in his first Annual Report as the suggestion of a madman capable of untold mischief.[21]

Yet the government accepted Hutton's first Annual Report, which was the most comprehensive up to that time.[22] In it Hutton condemned the state of the artillery, and pointed out the need for instructors, for the purchase of new equipment, and for the establishment of retirement pay. Above all he demanded that the respective duties of the General Officer Commanding and the Minister of Militia be clearly defined.

[18]Laurier Papers, Correspondence re Hutton, Laurier to Minto, June, 1899. The Prime Minister deemed it a painful duty "to bring to the attention of Your Excellency, a conflict which has just arisen between General Hutton and the Minister of Militia." Apparently the matter was temporarily smoothed over.

[19]Return 171, Aug. 11, 1899.

[20]John Buchan, Lord Minto (London, 1924), 127.

[21]A few years later Hutton actually wrote that Canada would need a force of 500,000 men to defend her border ("The Bond of Military Unity," a chapter in The Empire and the Century: A Series of Essays, London, 1905, 231).

[22]Buchan, Lord Minto, 128.

In spite of the growing opposition in the Cabinet, Hutton met with increasing success amongst the general public. The Toronto *Globe* enthusiastically wrote that there existed a "really wonderful degree of training which General Hutton has managed to impart to the troops."[23] Lord Minto wrote of his success to Lord Wolseley that "the country itself is very military in feeling and he [Hutton] has struck a right note, with the result that the people and the press generally are on his side."[24] But Hutton's greatest triumph in Canada was yet to come.

III

Under the compulsion of public opinion the Canadian government in October, 1899, reluctantly agreed to requests from the British authorities to despatch troops to South Africa. That outcome was remarkable in view of the blunt opposition of Sir John A. Macdonald, only fourteen years before, to sending troops to the Sudan.[25] In the period just prior to the war three influences were at work moulding public opinion: first, efficient propaganda flowing from sources controlled by Rhodes's interests; secondly, the activities of Canadian imperialists, such as Lieutenant-Colonel Sam Hughes; thirdly, the actions of the British government and its agents who "led" or "pressed" Canada to send troops.

Although Hutton did not play a sensational part in Canada's entry into the South African War, yet his frequent speeches advocating a "national army," which would rally in the Empire's hour of need, were of vital importance. In the few months preceding the outbreak he also laid careful plans for the organization of an official contingent, at the same time blocking a scheme to enlist a Canadian brigade in the British army.

A volunteer brigade was one of the three possibilities facing the Canadian government. The organization of such a brigade might allow the Canadian government to escape official participation. But the full might of the British Empire at bay could only be exerted through the unanimous agreement of all the colonies; consequently each colony had to support or be induced to support official participation—the second possibility. Theoretically the Canadian government need not have given official sanction to any troops sent abroad. Indeed that was what Lord

[23]June 21, 1899.
[24]Buchan, *Lord Minto*, 129-30, April 21, 1899.
[25]Macdonald to Tupper, March 12, 1885, in Sir Joseph Pope, *Correspondence of Sir John Macdonald* (Toronto, 1921), 338.

Minto and General Hutton desperately feared.   Actually, of course, the British authorities merely by refusing to accept volunteers helped to force the Canadian government officially to despatch troops.   If, however, the Canadian government had made careful preparations, it is possible that neutrality might have been the third possibility for the first two months of the war.   But the Cabinet had no policy except drift and avoidance of commitments. To Laurier and his colleagues South Africa was a country far away bristling with problems of no concern to Canada.   Participation in war was simply a subject that need not even be considered. That is not to say that Canada could have avoided sending troops, for the forces of imperialism were far too well organized and the public was deeply interested in the fortunes of Britain.   Even if the government had succeeded in keeping Canada out of the South African War then, two months later it would have failed to resist the tide of feeling that mounted as a result of the three British defeats in "Black Week." On the other hand, if the government had foreseen the course of events and attempted to guide them, it need not have suffered the damaging loss of prestige and might also have spared Canada the worst of the race quarrels that plagued the country during the war.   Instead the government did nothing except keep its hands untied.   Hence the real struggle took place between Hutton, who determined that Canada should send an official force, and Lieutenant-Colonel Sam Hughes, who for years had set his heart on enlisting and leading a Canadian brigade of volunteers in the British army.[26]

Prior to the end of August, 1899, Hughes had been content to write increasingly heated letters to Hutton demanding the General's acceptance of his plan of volunteers.[27] But rumours concerning an official force of soldiers to serve in South Africa carefully circulated by Hutton among military men and planted in the press galvanized Hughes into action.   He now turned to the Prime Minister, only to find him completely negative as well. For Hutton, apparently aware of Laurier's reluctance to permit Canadian troops to serve abroad, and aware too of his indifference regarding British hints for troops, told the Prime Minister that Canadians "would not go; were not wanted, and if they went,

[26]Cf. Hughes's motion in *Canada, House of Commons Debates*, May 1, 1899, 2335-56.
[27]*Canada, Sessional Papers*, Return 77 . . . for copies of all correspondence . . . between Major-General Hutton and Lieutenant-Colonel Samuel Hughes, M.P. . . . Feb. 19, 1900.

they would be a 'menace'."[28] By this slur on the fighting ability
of Canadians it is likely that Hutton wished to forestall any
government statement that might compromise his own maturing
scheme.[29] This reported insult so rebuffed Hughes that he forthwith decided to force Canada to send troops by writing a letter
to the press in which he called for the names of volunteers willing
to go to South Africa.[30] The widespread response to Hughes's
appeal so alarmed Hutton that he now resorted to every means at
his disposal to discredit Hughes's scheme. In part he succeeded.
He prevented the despatching of an unofficial volunteer force,
but not of volunteers as part of an official force.

Meanwhile the opposition to Hughes and the exact rumours
in the press gave rise to the belief in the Cabinet that General
Hutton had secretly recruited troops behind its back.[31] No
evidence has been adduced to prove this, for it was the object of
the British authorities not to obtain colonial troops, but to gain
official support. Yet it is easy to understand how the idea arose
after the acceptance by the Colonial Secretary of offers never
made[32] and especially after Hutton's premeditated visit to the
Honourable R. J. Scott, a bitter opponent of the General, to
inform him that public opinion would compel the government to
despatch troops, a view angrily denied by the Minister.[33] This
provocative action took place just prior to his deliberately ab-
senting himself from Ottawa for the ostentatious purpose of
making an inspection tour of the West in order to avoid the
appearance of trying to coerce the government. Upon his departure a carefully organized propaganda campaign by the Montreal
Star began whipping opinion into a frenzy.[34] The Boer ultimatum
to Queen Victoria now made further government inaction impossible.

The government blamed Hutton for placing its members in
an awkward dilemma, but since Lord Minto and General Hutton
together had made organizational plans, the government dared not

[28]Hughes's Papers, formerly in the possession of the late Major-General Garnet
Hughes, An Unfinished Autobiography (1921?), 54; and Memorandum "Re Friction
between Colonel Hughes and General Hutton culminating in 1900." There is no indication of the date of the latter except that it is before 1912.
[29]Cf. Laurier's statement of October 3, 1899, arguing that Canada could not send
troops to South Africa. But that utterance was made far too late, for it provoked the
very agitation it wished to quiet.
[30]Canada, House of Commons Debates, Feb. 25, 1901, 403-4.
[31]Buchan, Lord Minto, 137.
[32]Laurier Papers, Laurier Scrapbook, 78, Minto to Chamberlain, Oct. 12, 1899.
[33]Buchan, Lord Minto, 137.
[34]Vide Norman Penlington, "Canada's Entry into the Boer War" (unpublished
Master's Thesis, University of Toronto Library, 1937), 132-6.

lift its hand against the General for something in which the Governor-General had assisted. Nor did it dare run counter to the initial flood of war enthusiasm then at high tide. But the government did not forget, it merely awaited the opportune moment to rid itself of Hutton.

IV

It had not long to wait. The three British defeats in "Black Week," December, 1899, delivered a shattering blow to British prestige. The shrill cry "The Empire is in danger," which insisted on a greater Canadian war effort, could not drown the chorus of jeers over what many Canadians considered the stupid inability of the British soldier to adjust himself quickly to the tactics of the wily enemy. When the Minister of Militia could openly taunt Hutton with, "I ask myself in face of the reverses which the British army has received, if it is worth the while of Canada to remain part of the Empire,"[35] Laurier need no longer fear any public anger at the discharge of the General.

The immediate occasion for his recall grew out of the friction arising from three incidents: first, from the organization of the Second Contingent; secondly, from that of the Strathcona Horse; and thirdly, from the startling discovery of secret instructions to officials of the Militia Department.

Early in January, 1900, the government gave Hutton the task of forming a regiment of mounted infantrymen—the Second Contingent.[36] To obtain the horses required for such a large number of men, Hutton on his own responsibility appointed a committee under Colonel Kitson, Commandant of the Royal Military College, to supervise purchases.[37] Suspecting that such a committee would show partiality to Conservative horse dealers, the Minister of Militia insisted on the appointment of a Liberal member of parliament to the committee to report on the purchases. Over this episode Hutton received several rude letters.[38] Already aware, from the refusal of the government to grant him leave of absence in South Africa, that matters were rapidly moving to a crisis, he interviewed Laurier to find as he suspected that the Canadian authorities frowned on his activities.

At the same time Lord Strathcona, the Dominion High Commissioner in London, had appointed the General practically as his

[35]Buchan, *Lord Minto*, 149.
[36]S. B. Steele, *Forty Years in Canada* (Toronto, 1915), 338.
[37]Memoranda of Lieutenant-Colonel F. Cummins.
[38]Buchan, *Lord Minto*, 146.

representative to raise, mount, and equip a regiment, which the
High Commissioner, who was a very wealthy man, had personally
presented to the imperial government.[39]   The alacrity with which
the Prime Minister placed the services of the Militia Department
at the High Commissioner's disposal, and the umbrage taken at
Strathcona's insistence on his force being kept non-political, shows
the determination of the Canadian government to keep a firm
hand on Hutton.   Hutton, desiring immediate instructions for the
organization of the Strathcona Horse, foresaw no difficulties if
"given a free hand."[40]   But it was impossible for the deadlock
between the Minister and the General to continue any longer.

Laurier laboured under no illusions as to the difficulties of
getting rid of Hutton.   Although the government knew Hutton
was a personal aide-de-camp to the Queen and was supported by
all the power of the British authorities, yet it was determined to
administer a decisive check against all imperialism that brazenly
attempted to circumscribe Canada's powers.   The recall of Hutton
would best serve that purpose.

The strategy of the Governor-General in the coming three-
weeks' struggle was to gain time by delay and to consult with the
British authorities.   The Prime Minister, needlessly fearing public
opinion, followed a strategy of patient and wary persuasiveness
until the discovery of Hutton's secret instructions to officials of
the Militia Department made the question of recall urgent.

From the beginning, the interviews between Laurier and Minto
seem to have been heated and stormy, certainly on Minto's side.
In the first interview before January 20, Sir Wilfred Laurier demanded Hutton's recall on the ground, Buchan claims, merely of
want of tact.   But Laurier wrote sharply to Strathcona that
Hutton "was meddlesome, ignores the authority of the Minister,
and constantly acts as one who holds himself independent of civil
authority."[41]   Later, when Hutton was safely recalled, he qualified
that judgment by admitting that he was "in many respects . . . a
meritorious officer, painstaking, enthusiastic and very much in
love with his profession."[42]   In reply Minto took a very strong
line: he warmly upheld Hutton's actions, contending that were
the Militia Department free of politics, Hutton could do good
work.   He added that in transmitting the request for recall he
would feel compelled to place his own opinion before the Colonial

[39]Beckles Willson, *Life of Lord Strathcona* (London, 1915), 519.
[40]Laurier Papers, Correspondence re Hutton, Hutton to Laurier, Jan. 22, 1900.
[41]Laurier Papers, Laurier Scrapbook, Feb. 1, 1900, Very Confidential.
[42]Laurier Papers, Correspondence re Hutton, Laurier to Strathcona, Feb. 22, 1900.

Secretary, a practice which the Governor-General frequently followed. Such an action, the Prime Minister retorted, might compel his government's resignation. Undaunted, Minto wrote to Chamberlain that he would accept its resignation.[43]

After the next warm interview on January 20, Minto stated his views somewhat strongly in a memorandum which, Minto claimed, fell accidentally into all the Cabinet's hands instead of into those of a committee of the Cabinet. It protested against political interference in the Department of Militia and against Dr. Borden's behaviour and discourtesy.[44] The Cabinet drew up a long and heated constitutional discourse in reply which, Buchan claims, Minto accepted but considered irrelevant. But the strength and tenor of the Cabinet's answer must have nettled him, for the greater part of his letter in reply consisted of a virtual apology and a watering down of opinion. After pointing out that the problem was one of a "broad view of the position of *a* Minister and *a* General Officer Commanding" and that "in the special case of the purchase of horses the Minister's action appears out of accordance with the intentions of Militia Regulations and military custom," the Governor-General intimated that he was "far from wishing to appear as opposing Dr. Borden" and was "really sorry that the confidential memo" should have been placed "before council." He regretted "if its somewhat strong sentences should have appeared too critical."[45] On the same day Laurier denied that Minto had specified that only a committee of the Cabinet was to see the memorandum. He countered that "he thought its language very strong," but that he had openly declared that the views "you strenuously urged upon me" and had "set down" would be faithfully reported "to Council."[46] Minto's explanations and excuses on the errant memorandum have the reminiscent ring of the misquoted politician.

Laurier had hitherto followed a policy of caution. Now he telegraphed to Strathcona to inform Chamberlain that it was "urgent that General be recalled."[47] What brought the note of urgency into Laurier's calculations was the discovery of the downright insubordination of Hutton. Unknown to the Minister, the General had adopted a year earlier two sets of orders: (1) those to be passed on by the Minister, (2) those which he considered himself competent to issue and which were not referred to the

[43]Buchan, *Lord Minto*, 146-7.
[44]*Ibid.*, 147.
[45]Laurier Papers, Correspondence re Hutton, Minto to Laurier, Feb. 3, 1900.
[46]*Ibid.*, Laurier to Minto, Feb. 3, 1900.
[47]Laurier Papers, Laurier Scrapbook, Feb. 5, 1900.

Minister.   Under this scheme, even while his recall was being
considered, Hutton appointed and published a list of ten candidates to take the first staff course held for Canadian officers.   The
Minister of Militia, on seeing the list after publication, stroked
out the names of Lieutenant-Colonels White and Vince.   A letter
signed by Colonel S. Foster, the Chief Staff Officer, "by order of
the Major General Commanding" informed Lieutenant-Colonel
White that he could not take the course because of "his having
recently taken an active part in politics by public speaking."[48]
The Tory press gleefully published this letter.

Trying to undo the damaging effect of Hutton's provocative
letter, the Minister himself wrote to Lieutenant-Colonel White
explaining that it had been decided that "the course should be
given to younger men."   On Dr. Borden's request that Colonel
Foster should come to answer for his conduct and produce a copy
of the offending letter to Lieutenant-Colonel White, he refused.
The Minister's amazement turned to anger on learning later that
both he and Colonel Aylmer, the Adjutant-General, were acting
under the strict and secret orders of Major-General Hutton not
to show the Minister any papers, nor permit him to sign any, nor
even to see him, without the General's permission being first
obtained.   If perforce either of them had dealings with Dr.
Borden he was straightway to inform the General of what had
happened.[49]   No wonder Laurier wrote that affairs in the Department had come to a standstill and that the fact that "he is
no longer acceptable to the Canadian Government should be
sufficient for his prompt recall."[50]

The Governor-General now had to agree to Hutton's recall,
but tried to make the recall official so that the government might
bear full public responsibility for its actions.   This action was
necessary, he maintained, "because of the departure from Canada
of previous generals on no recognized official grounds."[51]   In this
he succeeded, although strongly opposed by both Laurier and
Chamberlain: Laurier, ostensibly because he wanted to settle the
difficulty without reflecting on the General, but more likely because he feared to add any more fat to the flames of racial and
imperialist controversy then raging fiercely; Chamberlain, because
"an official publication of correspondence would not serve a useful purpose."[52]

[48]Jan. 26, 1900, quoted in *Canada, House of Commons Debates*, April 3, 1900, 3077.
[49]*Ibid.*, 3097.
[50]Laurier Papers, Laurier Scrapbook, Feb. 1, 1900, Very Confidential.
[51]Laurier Papers, Correspondence re Hutton, Minto to Laurier, Feb. 6, 1900.
[52]Laurier Papers, Laurier Scrapbook, report of letter from Chamberlain, Strathcona
to Laurier, Feb. 13, 1900, 136.

Meanwhile Hutton, not yet recalled or dismissed, decided to cast caution to the winds and actually proposed to the Governor-General to ask for a Royal Commission "to report upon the administration of the Department of Militia and Defence . . . and consider the relative position of the Minister of Militia and the General Officer Commanding . . ."[53] His recall two days later cut short that proposal. Not even then could he resist one last fling at the government. On February 14, the day before leaving Canada, at a banquet held in his honour he publicly attacked the government for political interference in Militia affairs.[54]

Laurier had judged the proper time of Hutton's recall far better than he could have foreseen, for Hutton's remarks had surprisingly little echo, either amongst the public or in parliament. Interest in the South African War and the tarnished reputation of British generals no doubt kept the issue quiet; moreover, the public, having little love for Hutton since his quarrel with Hughes, believed unjustifiably that General Hutton had prevented Colonel Hughes from being the commander of the contingent from mere personal spite. The most important cause of public apathy probably was the ostensible reason put forward that Hutton had received a "recall for active service." Laurier, in reply to charges of politics in the Militia Department, explained that the causes of the differences were "that General Hutton was insubordinate and indiscreet and deliberately ignored the authority of the administration of the department." Any General Officer Commanding, he continued, "on accepting the position in question becomes from that time an officer in the employment of and subject in all respects to the government of Canada."[55]

One important result of Hutton's departure was the revival of agitation in all Canadian circles, both imperialist and nationalist, for the appointment of a Canadian General Officer Commanding, a course which apparently Lord Minto thought the government intended following. The British authorities emphatically protested[56] and the Canadian government agreed on the ground that it felt the time had not arrived for such a change of policy.[57]

Both the British and Canadian authorities stoutly maintained their positions for and against Hutton's conduct. Chamberlain

[53]Laurier Papers, Correspondence re Hutton, Feb. 8, 1900.
[54]Ottawa *Citizen*, Feb. 15, 1900.
[55]*Canada, House of Commons Debates*, Feb. 19, 1900, 595-6.
[56]Public Archives of Canada, Confidential Despatches, Colonial Office, Chamberlain to Minto, April 9, 1900.
[57]Laurier Papers, Laurier Scrapbook, Minto to Chamberlain, April 14, 1900, 177.

wrote that he received the minute explaining the Cabinet's action with regret. Keenly disappointed that Hutton and his two predecessors could not complete their work he became aware of a permanent cause of the difficulty, which he only dared hint at. Her Majesty's Government had appointed "experts in military administration and of course, absolutely removed from political influence." Although recognizing that "the responsibility to Parliament must be maintained" yet it was desirable that a General Officer Commanding "should have a freer hand in matters essential to the discipline and efficiency of the Militia. . . ." Finally he practically conceded the main contention of the Canadian government when he wrote that the officers deserved favourable consideration if in their zeal for the thorough efficiency of the forces, they had at times appeared not fully to appreciate local conditions.[58]

In a memorandum in reply Dr. Borden at great length defended the government's position. He denied that the recall was due to political causes. Such a state of affairs he blandly assumed "has not within his knowledge prevailed and does not prevail in Canada." Fortunately he could rest the case of the government on far stronger grounds. He outlined in great detail Hutton's disobedience to instructions, his attempts to dictate to the Minister, his indiscretions, and above all the shocking incident of secret instructions to subordinate officials in the Militia Department.[59] The British government could not reply to that.

V

Although the Canadian government had dramatically upheld its autonomy, it would never again be able to ignore the problems posed by imperialism: it could no longer hold back the defence expenditure nor block the continuous improvement of the Militia. For the rivalry of empires was soon to plunge mankind into war and the "vortex of militarism." It was certain that Britain, a source of investment and a market of Canadian goods, was bound to be involved. The realization of that fact and its implications for the continued prosperity of the Dominion forced Canada farther along the path first openly pointed out more than forty years ago by General Hutton.

[58]Confidential Despatches, C. O., Chamberlain to Minto, April 17, 1900.
[59]Laurier Papers, Correspondence re Hutton, Memorandum of the Minister of Militia on confidential despatch of the Right Honourable Secretary of State for Colonies of April 17, 1900.

The Round Table Movement in Canada, 1909-1920

JAMES EAYRS

ACCORDING to its founder, Lionel Curtis, the Round Table movement arose from the perplexity of some of the members of Milner's Kindergarten upon finding themselves citizens of the new South Africa they had helped to create. "Not to know or to be able to explain what kind of citizenship was ours seemed to us an intolerable condition. . . . We determined, therefore, to investigate the whole subject and not rest from inquiry until we had discovered what, in fact, as citizens of a Dominion we now were; whether that citizenship was one with which free men should rest content and, if not, what were the changes in our condition that we were called upon to seek." The inquirers—Curtis, Philip Kerr, and William Marris—turned first to Canada, "because Canadians were the people who had lived longest in the same position as that we had just attained in South Africa," and in 1909 they talked with leading men in the Dominion about its present and future status. They found little of their own perplexity: to most Canadians "the difficulties which presented themselves to us were academic." There was general agreement that the proper course was for the Dominions each in their own way to assume control of their external affairs. Common sentiment and common interest would hold together an Empire of fully autonomous communities.[1]

Curtis, on his return to England, analysed this view and found it unsatisfying. Suppose Pretoria to be at peace when London was at war. Would foreign governments accept and respect its position? That was unlikely. But if they did, the dilemma as he saw it remained. For a Dominion to differ from the mother country on the great issue of peace or war might be a solution, but "a solution which meant the undoing of all those ideals for which the people of the Empire had fought, suffered and won, in South Africa."[2] The only

*I am grateful to the Executors of the Estate of Sir Edmund Walker for permission to use the Walker Papers deposited at the Library of the University of Toronto; to Mrs. C. H. A. Armstrong of Toronto and Professor Dennis H. Wrong of Brown University for permission to use the G. M. Wrong Papers also deposited at the Library of the University of Toronto; and to G. P. de T. Glazebrook, Esq., of Ottawa for permission to use the correspondence of A. J. Glazebrook. My thanks are due to Miss M. E. Brown, Head of the Rare Books and Special Collections Department of the Library of the University of Toronto, for her help while consulting the Walker Papers and the Wrong Papers.

[1]Lionel Curtis, "The Round Table Movement: Its Past and Future," Address before the Round Table Society of Toronto, Nov. 18, 1913, 10–12.

[2]*Ibid.*, 12.

Reprinted from *Canadian Historical Review*, XXXVIII (1), March, 1957

solution thus proved on closer inspection to be intolerable. Co-operation, the alternative which the Canadian inquiry had shown to be "so prevalent as to be almost universal," was "no genuine alternative but only a sham one which served to conceal the real issues." Continued dependence was equally chimerical. The real alternatives were two, "and two only, between which the States of the Empire would have to choose—independence, or organic union."[3]

These views Curtis embodied in a Memorandum, and because they were "so obviously distasteful to public opinion" he thought it well to submit them "to the criticism of thoughtful people in the other Dominions."[4] New Zealand was first to be selected, perhaps because it had been in that Dominion that the project of imperial federation had found most support.[5] Early in 1911 he visited Canada again, this time to organize study groups. Professor G. M. Wrong of the University of Toronto was one of a number to whom Curtis explained his plans at a dinner at the York Club on February 15, 1911:

A Committee in each of the Divisions of Greater Britain is working on the problem of finding out the common interests of the various parts of the British Empire and the possibility of organization to meet them. At present we think that Defence, and flowing from it, Foreign Affairs, exhaust the interest that we all have in common. Curtis asked me to act as the Chairman of the Toronto Committee to make the study of this part of the Canadian problem. About twenty of us are engaged in the study. If we can achieve anything our gathering to-night will be epoch-making in the history of the world. On beginnings so slight do great issues sometimes depend.[6]

Soon groups were meeting regularly in Toronto and in Montreal.[7] Their discussion, as a later Round Table pamphlet was careful to point out, was not confined to Curtis's Memorandum; but in fact a

[3]*Round Table Studies*, Series I, no. 1, xv.

[4]*Ibid.*, xvi–xvii.

[5]Keith Sinclair, *Imperial Federation: A Study of New Zealand Policy and Opinion 1880–1914* (London, 1955, Commonwealth Paper no. 2). See pp. 42–4 for an account of the influence of the New Zealand Round Table movement on Sir Joseph Ward at the Imperial Conference of 1911.

[6]Wrong Papers, Diary, entry of Feb. 15, 1911.

[7]Among the original members of the Toronto group were Professor G. M. Wrong of the University's Department of History; Professor Edward Kylie, also of that Department; Sir Edmund Walker, President of the Canadian Bank of Commerce; and A. J. Glazebrook. Kylie was a young man of brilliance and promise who was elected President of the Oxford Debating Union, "a dignity conferred for the first time on a colonial." H. J. Morgan, *Canadian Men and Women of the Time* (Toronto, 1912), 623. He died in 1916, of typhoid while training with the Canadian Army. Arthur Glazebrook during this phase of his life-long association with the Canadian Round Table movement was an exchange broker in Toronto. He was a close friend of Lord Milner. It was to his initiative and industry that the Canadian Round Table movement largely owed whatever influence it had during the period examined in this paper.

close and careful scrutiny of that document, which they called "the Green Memorandum" (presumably on account of the colour of its binding), or, more familiarly, "the Egg,"[8] was their first and main order of business. They dissected the Green Memorandum sentence by sentence, recording their observations in marginal notes. These comments, together with more general observations, were sent to Curtis in England. The material thus furnished by the groups in the Dominions represented the views of seventy-five critics. Towards the end of 1911 Curtis prepared an edition of the Green Memorandum with their comments printed on the pages opposite the texts to which they referred. The result was the so-called "Annotated Memorandum," a volume of some 800 pages. It was privately printed,[9] and circulated among the members of the Round Table groups pending the production of yet another report by Curtis in which the argument of the Green Memorandum was to be re-examined in the light of the comments of the critics.

It was Curtis's intention to distil this report from the Annotated Memorandum "in about six months"—which, as he later confessed, was an "absurdly wrong" estimate. "Not six months but more like three years was needed for the task I had undertaken, and to accomplish it in that time it was necessary to act less as a draughtsman than as an editor, and to enlist the expert assistance of as many other members of the Round Table as possible."[10] Three more volumes resulted. The first of these was Part One of *The Project of a Commonwealth*, in Curtis's words "an attempt to show how and why the British Commonwealth came into being."[11] Part Two followed; it was "a survey of each of the different countries included in the great Commonwealth, conducted with a view to seeing what kind of community it has become by reason of its position and also to gauge what its position is." Part Three was somewhat different. It dealt with the future; and was "prepared in such a way that it will stand alone and can be read by itself by those who cannot afford the time to follow the track of the inquiry through the second and third volumes." Here was the heart of the matter. Curtis was asked by

[8]Walker Papers, Journal, I, 327, entry of July 6, 1911. "9 a.m. Bkfst. with Mr L. Curtis to discuss his Imperial plans—the printed form of which—called The Egg—is being discussed by many."

[9]As *Round Table Studies*, Series I, no. 1. A second volume, dealing in the same way with Australia, was printed in 1914.

[10]Curtis, "Round Table Movement," 20.

[11]It was prepared in five installments of which four were completed before World War I. Each was printed and circulated among the Round Table groups as it was finished. In the light of their criticisms the complete text was prepared and at the close of 1914 issued for private circulation as *The Project of a Commonwealth, Part I*. It was offered to the public in 1916 as *The Commonwealth of Nations*.

the Round Table in Canada and in the United Kingdom to make its argument available in rough draft pending the completion of a more polished version. He agreed, and circulated in August, 1914, *A Practical Enquiry into the Nature of Citizenship in the British Empire and into the Relation of its Several Communities to Each Other*—the so-called "Strawberry Memorandum." It was a preliminary version of *The Problem of the Commonwealth* which appeared privately in 1915 and then was published as a public document in circumstances which will be discussed below.

This programme of private study and discussion of documents was one of two ways by which the work of the Round Table movement was carried out in its initial stage. The other was by publishing a quarterly magazine. The nature of this enterprise was sketched in a memorandum by Philip Kerr early in 1910. "What is wanted is a quarterly review, severely detached from the domestic party issues of the day, and written anonymously with the sole aim of exchanging information and ideas about the imperial problem." It should be published where there was the best access to the best news—"clearly London, which is also the nerve centre of the Empire." It was to be called "The Moot," or "The Round Table." It was not intended to seek out a mass readership "by popular methods or flag-wagging"; only those "genuinely interested in the problem of imperial organization" were to be invited to subscribe. A quota of 300 such subscribers was set for each Dominion, for "unless it can be ensured that practically all men of real influence in politics, journalism, business, etc., who are in any way sympathetic, subscribe . . . , it is not worth while making a start."[12] Sir Edmund Walker was asked to round up Canadian subscribers. He agreed, and duly reached his quota. Although sympathetic to the project, his enthusiasm was not unrestrained:

After all it will come to the question of whether the magazine can be made really interesting or not. We have now the Journal of the Royal Colonial Institute, the magazine called National Defence, the colonial edition of The Standard . . . , the colonial edition of the Weekly Times, and many other publications devoted to Imperialism. I do not find any of these very interesting. . . . A quarterly journal of the character of the great reviews would certainly be valuable to Imperialism, but one wonders whether it could have a wide enough range of interest while serving only one main purpose.[13]

Volume I, number 1 of *The Round Table: A Quarterly Review of the Politics of the British Empire* appeared in November of 1910.

[12]Walker Papers, copy of undated memorandum by Philip Kerr.
[13]*Ibid.*, Sir Edmund Walker to A. J. Glazebrook, May 10, 1910.

It contained an article on Anglo-German rivalry, and pieces on the local political scene from correspondents in Britain and South Africa. The Canadian correspondent furnished brief essays on Sir Wilfrid Laurier and Tariff Revision, Imperial Co-operation, and Parties and the Navy. An Introductory Note promised "a regular account of what is going on throughout the King's Dominions, written with first-hand knowledge and entirely free from the bias of local political issues." "*The Round Table*," it declared, "does not aim at propounding new theories or giving voice to ingenious speculations. It will serve its purpose if it contributes to the better understanding of the problems of the Empire and to their solution, and if no one ever raises the charge against it that it has distorted the truth for its own ends."[14]

It was not long, however, before just such a charge was being raised in Canada. [14a] "I know," wrote Rodolphe Lemieux, a former Cabinet Minister,

that many Canadian liberals are members of the Round Table—I, for one, am a reader of the periodical . . . *but* reading it as I do I have come to the conclusion that it is a jingo institution. . . . I find that almost all of the contributions on Canada are tainted with ardent toryism. . . . The articles on South Africa are biased. The stalwart imperialists do not realize what are the difficulties of Botha—the best friend of England in the dark continent. They did not realize what were Laurier's troubles. Their aim was to destroy Laurier *by all means*, so as to defeat Asquith afterwards. . . . Such are the impressions I gather after reading the *Round Table*. There is an *inner circle* in that organization—I know it, *I feel it*. Of course he [Lionel Curtis] is one of Milner's disciples—he belongs to the *Knitergarten* [*sic*] and for me, such associations have a strong tory-jingo flavor.[15]

Another Liberal, the editor of the *Toronto Star*, conceded that the *Round Table* was

well-written and sometimes shows a surprising breadth of view. But it is useless to disguise the fact that the Round Tablers want to create a new Parliament which will have the power to tax Canada, in return for what they call a "voice" in foreign affairs. My own notion is that the voice would be about as powerful as mine would be if they appointed me a director of the Bank of Commerce. I would strut about, full of vanity, but I would have no real influence.[16]

[14]The *Round Table*, I, no. 1, Nov. 15, 1910, 2, 5–6.
[14a]And in India. See Lionel Curtis, "A Letter to the People of India," reprinted in Lionel Curtis, *Dyarchy* (London, 1920), 38–90.
[15]Wrong Papers, Rodolphe Lemieux to G. M. Wrong, Aug. 29, 1913.
[16]P.A.C., Willison Papers, 18625–30, John Lewis to Sir John Willison, Feb. 16, 1916.

By others the charge of duplicity and, indeed, of conspiracy was levelled against the Round Table's study groups. "The Round Tables," wrote the editor of the *Montreal Herald*, "are kept in close touch with the directing minds in England. Is it beyond belief that there is a machinery in existence which can cause speeches to be made, in Great Britain, and other things to happen, when needed, which will help maintain a continuity of interest? To think otherwise would be to withhold from very capable men who are making this their life's work the admiration that is their due."[17] To Laurier himself there was no doubt. "Canada," he wrote in 1917, "is now governed by a junta sitting at London, known as 'The Round Table,' with ramifications in Toronto, in Winnipeg, in Victoria, with Tories and Grits receiving their ideas from London and insidiously forcing them on their respective parties."[18] J. W. Dafoe offered, in a private letter, a more detailed indictment:

I have no doubt that the Canadian Round Table circles are precisely what you describe them to be, an organization for inquiry; but I have never regarded the members of the movement in London as other than protagonists of a somewhat clearly defined idea. I have considered their assumption of the open mind as, to put it frankly, lacking in candour. They have had from the outset the intention that the inquiry should result in the apparent endorsement of their own scheme for Empire consolidation, which they have held from the beginning. What Mr Curtis is advocating now as the claimed result of years of inquiry he believed in and advocated some years ago. . . . I have regarded the Canadian members of the Round Table as persons who were being shepherded along a definite path to a predetermined end, and I have thought that many of them were thus being shepherded so skillfully that they realized neither the road that [they] were travelling, nor the goal to which they were tending. . . .[19]

What truth is there in these charges?

II

The Round Table movement professed to hold aloof from politics. "In an enterprise like this," Lionel Curtis had written, "there is little room for the management of parties, or for political chess play of any kind."[20] He had specifically advised the Canadian group to keep out of the political arena. While "individual members of the Round Table are as free as air to support whichever policy they think best,"

[17]Joseph C. Walsh, *Moccasin Prints*, no. 1 (Montreal, 1913).
[18]Quoted in O. D. Skelton, *The Life and Letters of Sir Wilfrid Laurier* (Toronto, 1921), II, 510.
[19]Wrong Papers, J. W. Dafoe to G. M. Wrong, Oct. 16, 1916.
[20]*Round Table Studies*, Series I, no. 1, 392.

he saw "no justification for the organization, as a whole, doing so. . . . Once let the association enter that field it will close against itself its own proper field—that of educating public opinion on matters which are not as yet the subject of party controversies and ought never to become so."[21] Yet while the Canadian Round Table did not itself intervene, its leading members did, often in consultation with or at the suggestion of the London group. It thus became neither easy nor accurate to maintain that the movement was always above the fray when its members were themselves so deeply involved.

Their earliest move at "political chess" concerned the possibility of obtaining permanent representation for the Dominions on the Committee of Imperial Defence. When certain members of the British Government appeared to favour such a policy, Lionel Curtis wrote immediately to G. M. Wrong in Toronto. He urged its advantages, and suggested that the Round Table should carry an article in its support. Arrangements should be made for Borden to receive a copy in advance of publication and "for lengthy extracts to be produced and reviewed in Canadian papers the moment the Round Table comes out." Its appearance in the Round Table, Curtis concluded, would mean "that the article thus becomes simultaneously current throughout all the Dominions and tends to make Australia, New Zealand and South Africa follow your lead."[22] Wrong replied that Glazebrook, Kylie, himself, and Sir Edmund Walker—who was "looming up more and more as a leading man—I had him indeed in mind as a possible member of the Defence Committee"—had talked the matter over but had decided that "by the time the article came out the question might be practically settled." To Curtis's suggestion that Stephen Leacock should write the article Wrong responded: "In any case we rather doubted whether it would be quite safe to have the article prepared in the manner you suggested. Willison is ready to prepare the article, if it is thought wise to have one, and you know the vigour of his pen."[23] Curtis acquiesced. An article in the September, 1912, number referred to the proposed permanent representation of the Dominions as "a Council of Ministers from the united nations of the Empire . . . not a true Cabinet of Empire, [but] . . . a great step beyond anything in existence at present."[24] Whether the three or four pages thus employed

[21]Curtis, "Round Table Movement," 42.
[22]Wrong Papers, Lionel Curtis to G. M. Wrong, April 12, 1912.
[23]Ibid., G. M. Wrong to Lionel Curtis, May 22, 1912.
[24]The Round Table, no. 8, Sept., 1912, 635–6.

were in fulfilment of Curtis's suggestion or whether they were an alternative is not clear. At any rate the question was not settled at the time of their appearance.[25]

While this discussion was in progress, the London Round Table was corresponding with the Canadian group on the naval question. G. M. Wrong reported to Lionel Curtis that the Borden Government was disposed to offer very considerable assistance to the Admiralty:

> . . . The Conservative "workers" are beginning to see that a striking naval policy is "good politics." Nationalism in Quebec is practically dead and the Quebec Liberals, who are still supreme in the Province, are committed to a forward naval policy. The Liberals in Ontario are taking the same tone. . . . The result is that if the Government takes a strong line the support of this in both parties will be overwhelming. There is, indeed, a chance that the naval question may be taken out of party politics.
>
> . . . The present situation could not be more satisfactory from our point of view. Borden, who is developing considerable personal strength, will go to England soon. Hazen, the Minister directly concerned with the naval policy, is proving one of the strong men of the Cabinet. They go with an open mind and they will be anxious to fit in with whatever policy the Admiralty prefers. I have reason to believe that they are ready to appoint a Canadian member of the Defence Committee and to undertake at once to supply two "Dreadnoughts" to the Imperial Navy. What they will offer, however, will depend very much upon what the Admiralty asks. Do what you can to get the Admiralty to ask what is *best*, and not merely what they think Canada will do. . . .[26]

Curtis answered: "I can only reply to you in the words of Latimer, that this day you have lit a candle in Canada, which by God's help shall never be put out."[27]

To what extent Curtis and his friends in the Round Table movement in England were able to influence the framers of British policy in the direction desired by Wrong is not disclosed. But Curtis was able to catch Borden's ear and to have with him a "most instructive talk."[28] Wrong had prepared the way by writing to Borden before the latter's departure for England, telling him of the overwhelming sentiment for a "strong" naval policy that he and Edward Kylie had encountered during their recent trip across Canada.

---

[25]The right to be represented on the Committee of Imperial Defence when matters affecting them were under discussion was conceded to the Dominions, and between 1912 and the outbreak of war some Dominion ministers availed themselves of it. During the first months of the war the committee did not meet at all. See P.A.C., Borden Papers, Sir George Perley to Sir Robert Borden, Jan. 15, 1915.

[26]Wrong Papers, G. M. Wrong to Lionel Curtis, May 22, 1912.

[27]*Ibid.*, Lionel Curtis to G. M. Wrong, June 6, 1912.

[28]*Ibid.*, July 24, 1912.

The unanimity in regard to doing something effective was really striking. When I began to discuss details many people said they did not know enough about the question but were willing to trust the Canadian leaders. I found a good deal of doubt as to the wisdom of giving money or Dreadnoughts. This came chiefly from Liberals, and I think you would be attacked by the Liberals if you adopted this policy. I did not hear any objection to a plan for accepting full responsibility and partnership with Great Britain in respect to a fleet. "Grain-growers," some of whom I thought touched with fanaticism, were as emphatic in respect to this as were Conservative Imperialists. . . .[29]

As the result of their findings in the West, Wrong and Kylie began a movement to take the naval question out of party politics.[30] Philip Kerr, then in Toronto, reported to Lionel Curtis that the attempt "at present promises success. . . . To show how far the movement is genuine, I may say that Sir Edmund Walker on one side and Dafoe on the other, have agreed to further the scheme." He added that he himself had "not engineered this movement. . . . But I believe that success would materially advance the cause of organic union."[31]

Meeting in Winnipeg and Toronto, two groups of prominent citizens—the "Red parlour gang" as one disgruntled Liberal described them—eventually agreed upon the terms of a memorial, which it was proposed to circulate among the public and present to Borden and Laurier. It attempted to straddle the policies of the two parties by endorsing as a permanent policy "a navy worthy of our national aspirations," providing, however, that "if international relations as disclosed by official information are such as to indicate the existence of an urgent situation, substantial evidence should be given forthwith of Canada's recognition of her responsibilities as part of the Empire." It concluded by expressing the desirability of removing the question from party politics, and calling upon the Prime Minister to meet with the Leader of the Opposition to secure this end.[32]

Laurier was not pleased with the project. He had, he wrote to Dafoe, "no fault to find with our friends signing this memorial. The whole thing has been well arranged on our side. My question however was: why such a memorial at all? Why such an unusual proceeding? Why did not our friends reply, when approached, 'We have a policy and we stand by it'?"[33] Borden's immediate reaction

[29]Borden Papers, OC Series, file 652, G. M. Wrong to Sir Robert Borden, July 9, 1912.
[30]A different interpretation will be found in H. S. Ferns and B. Ostry, *The Age of Mackenzie King: The Rise of the Leader* (Toronto, 1955), 154 ff.
[31]Borden Papers, 7663–8, Philip Kerr to Lionel Curtis, July 31, 1912.
[32]Walker Papers, copy of undated memorandum.
[33]P.A.C., Dafoe Papers, Sir Wilfrid Laurier to J. W. Dafoe, Sept. 26, 1912.

to the memorial is not known to the present writer. But it is clear
that he was unmoved by its representations, for his naval policy,
announced at the end of the year, ignored that portion of it calling
for the creation of a Canadian navy. There was some dissatisfaction
at this outcome among the group which had organized the Toronto
meeting at the National Club on August 7, and a member of it
argued that those signatories of the memorial who had previously
supported Borden should now give their support to Laurier. This
suggestion was rejected by Edward Kylie, another member:

I do not consider that Mr Borden's policy is inconsistent with the Memorial. . . .
The present contribution comes fairly under the clause in the memorial which
relates to an emergency contribution. We had hoped, however, that the contribution should be accompanied by the establishment of a Canadian Fleet, and
it may be thought that on this ground we should oppose Mr Borden. Still it
seems only fair to notice that the permanent policy is not decided upon, that
Mr Borden's reason for not deciding upon it at present is that he must appeal
to the country upon this policy, and that the ships which are to be built are in
the control of Canada and can, if necessary, become later parts of a Canadian
fleet. . . .
    As to the general purpose of the Memorial, I am inclined to think that it was
never intended to be a club which the memorialists should use against the
Government or the Opposition. . . .[34]

Sir Edmund Walker agreed. "We shall," he wrote to Kylie, "of course
look with keen interest to Mr. Borden's proposals regarding the
establishment of an actual Navy, but this is a matter regarding which
we may not hear for some time."[35] So indeed it proved.

On only one further occasion did the members of the Round Table
movement in Canada attempt to shape the course of policy. During
the early months of the war, they tried to persuade the Government
to secure a meeting of the Imperial Conference. This project, like
that to secure Dominion representation on the Committee of Imperial Defence, originated with the London group. "The Round
Table in England," Edward Kylie wrote to Sir Edmund Walker
early in 1915,

is very keen that the Imperial Conference should go on this year as usual.
It would be a great sign to the Empire and to the world that we were
unanimous and imperturbable—and the very business with which the British
Ministers are at the moment engrossed is the kind which should be discussed
with the Overseas Premiers. Both Curtis and [Sir Edward] Peacock have
written urgently in this sense. I shall be most grateful if you will write Sir
Robert Borden and any other of the Ministers to support the idea of the
Conference.[36]

[34]Walker Papers, copy of Edward Kylie to John A. Cooper, Jan. 16, 1913.
[35]*Ibid.*, Sir Edmund Walker to Edward Kylie, Jan. 23, 1913.
[36]*Ibid.*, Edward Kylie to Sir Edmund Walker, Jan. 6, 1915.

Walker accordingly wrote to Borden, and a week later saw him in Ottawa where he was told that to hold the Imperial Conference that year would be "exceedingly difficult if not well-nigh impossible." This news Walker transmitted to Kylie, adding: "I wish I could say that I approve of the suggestion."[37] Although the London group was acquainted with the attitude of the Canadian Government, it was not persuaded to drop its advocacy of the project. "We have not abandoned it," one of its members wrote during the following month, "on the contrary I am sure that it is still extremely important." The London Round Table continued to press for the holding of the conference during 1915, but was not successful in this endeavour.

Such was the extent and nature of the attempt of the Round Table to influence Canadian policy; and it seems clear that Laurier's accusation that as "a junta sitting at London" it had come to govern Canada is less an accurate assessment of its influence than a measure of the extremes to which his usually serene mind had been driven by 1917.

In Dafoe's criticism, however, there is a good deal more force. From its inception there had been a marked ambiguity about the essential purpose of the Round Table movement. The inquiry was never presented to prospective or actual participants as a propagandist effort to implant the remedy of imperial federation in the minds of others. The project of organic union was discussed only as an agenda *raisonné*, a working hypothesis which impartial investigation might sustain or set aside. A movement engaged only in what one of its leading spirits termed "a propaganda of knowledge" might without compunction recruit members of every outlook. "There is no reason," G. M. Wrong had written to Dafoe, "why you with your views should not be a member of a Round Table group."[38]

Such was the theory. The practice was different. A movement devoted to impartial examination of the merits of organic union as a solution to the imperial problem was not likely to attract those who did not believe there was an imperial problem, still less those who wished to loosen the bonds of empire. The members of the Round Table groups in Canada were, with very few exceptions, those who favoured imperial federation as the ultimate if not immediate solution of the problem; and the exceptions were those who objected on grounds of practicability rather than of principle. Thus they were far from representing in even a vaguely proportionate way the mainstreams of Canadian opinion. The failure to secure the

37*Ibid.*, Sir Edmund Walker to Edward Kylie, Jan. 18, 1915.
38Dafoe Papers, G. M. Wrong to J. W. Dafoe, Sept. 20, 1916.

adhesion of more than one or two French-speaking members was particularly striking. Nor was this for want of trying.[39]

Moreover, the most active members, those who led and organized the movement, were precisely those who had arrived in their own minds at a very specific kind of solution and who were set fast against any alternative. Above all was this true of Lionel Curtis. And it was Curtis's intellect, energy, and productive pen which brought the movement into being and, having done so, gave it something to do. It was inevitable that his ideas should dominate its programme and that his influence should turn the propaganda of knowledge into propaganda for a federated empire.

This lightly veiled conflict of purpose was brought into the open by the publication in 1916 of Lionel Curtis's *The Problem of the Commonwealth*. Curtis's *Problem*, it will be recalled, had appeared late in 1915 in a privately printed edition which it was not intended to bring before the public until after the war.[40] Early in 1916, however, Curtis changed his mind in favour of immediate publication because the privately printed edition had been reviewed and portions printed out of context in the press. His decision was opposed with some heat by the Canadian Round Table. Its members feared that its proposals, particularly those dealing with powers of taxation with which Curtis had invested the Imperial Parliament, would alarm and alienate Canadian opinion, and do the Round Table movement in Canada immense harm. It was represented to Curtis that if he was determined to press forward with immediate publication the damage could be lessened if he added a preface stating that the financial proposals were highly tentative; or, better, if he were to publish only that portion of the book which dealt with the statement of the problem, omitting that portion which dealt with his solution.[41] A subsequent communication from the Round Table Council at Toronto suggested that this amended version should appear "under the name of the Round Table" rather than his own.[42]

Curtis did not take kindly to these suggestions. In a lengthy and well-reasoned letter he set forth his case for immediate publication

[39]Walker Papers, see data in file marked "Round Table"; also *ibid.*, Sir Edmund Walker to Sir George Garneau, Dec. 8, 1916.

[40]Borden Papers, OC Series, file 212, Lionel Curtis to Sir Robert Borden, Nov. 6, 1915.

[41]Walker Papers, copy, Secretary, Toronto Round Table Group, to Lionel Curtis, Feb. 21, 1916.

[42]*Ibid.*, March 2, 1916. A copy of this letter, together with a copy of Curtis's reply of March 28, 1916, is to be found in the small collection of Willison Papers deposited at the Archives of the Province of Ontario.

under his own name, for which he had the support of most of the London group, including Lord Milner who wrote to A. J. Glazebrook that "on the whole I think he may as well be allowed to open the ball in his own way."[43] There was, however, a division within the group as to whether it might not be advisable to water down the provisions for an imperial tax-gathering scheme which, as some of the Canadian members were urging most forcibly,[44] was anathema not only to the man in the street in Canada but to themselves. "There is a bit of a fuss," a member of the London group confided to his Canadian colleague, "with regard to the financial chapter. I have told Curtis that I agree with him, rather than with [R. H.] Brand and Philip Kerr, who appear to me to be of the ascetic kind and to want us all to put on hair shirts and feel the prickles just for the sake of feeling them, even though other clothing would suit the purpose of the weather just as well." And a few weeks later: "Several of the Round Table were against any modification, and I was one of the few who were in favour of it. I see no reason for making things stiffer than is necessary. One trouble about my friends of the R.T. is that they are all so serious and take themselves so. The issue of this book is something so momentous that it is debated as though the world were hanging on it."[45]

Eventually a compromise was reached. *The Problem* would be published under Curtis's name. There was to be a preface stating that the views expressed were those of the author alone and did not necessarily represent those of the Round Table movement. The financial chapter was emasculated in deference to the feelings of the Canadian membership. Curtis sailed for Canada to explain his decision personally to his Toronto friends.[46]

But as they had foreseen, the effect of the publication of *The Problem of the Commonwealth*, even in this amended version, was to expose the Round Table in Canada to a storm of hostile criticism. "There was some objection here," G. M. Wrong wrote to Dafoe, "to the publication of the book on the ground that the reader would not distinguish between Curtis's own views and those of the Round

[43]*Ibid.*, copy of Lionel Curtis to Secretary, Toronto Round Table Group, March 28, 1916. *Ibid.*, copy of Lord Milner to A. J. Glazebrook, March 8, 1916.
[44]For example, *ibid.*, A. J. Glazebrook to Philip Kerr, March 14, 1916; Sir Edmund Walker to Lord Milner, April 1, 1916.
[45]*Ibid.*, copies of Arthur Steel-Maitland to A. J. Glazebrook, Feb. 24, 1916; May 28, 1916.
[46]*Ibid.*, Journal, II, 125, entry of April 25, 1916. "Dinner at home for Curtis and the Round Table. . . . We had a long discussion ending in the conclusion that Curtis must publish, over his own name, a modified form of The Problem. . . ."

Table and this is precisely what has happened."[47] Sir Edmund
Walker wrote to a correspondent:

I am very much interested in what you say regarding the probability that the
average reader will suppose that Lionel Curtis's book represents the view of
the Round Table groups. This is a fear that those of us who are connected with
the Round Table have felt very much and are doing our best to correct. We
all respect and many of us love Lionel Curtis for his enthusiasm and for the
great scholarship he has shown in connection with the history of imperial and
Colonial development. We must not, however, forget that the Round Table
groups were established for the purpose of debate. . . . If the view of the
Round Table Council here could have prevailed Mr Curtis would only have
published that part of his book which has to do with history and not that part
which has to do with solutions. Most of us, I think, disagree with his conclusions
as to taxation, as to the control of India and the dependencies, and as to the
form of an Imperial Parliament. When he states that his book is the expression
of his personal opinion that is literally the truth because some of those associated
with him in England are more in agreement with our views than with his.[48]

III

The publication of Curtis's book and the misunderstandings there-
by created now suggested to the Canadian group that the time
had come for taking the public into its confidence. Hitherto its membership had been confined to a select few; no attempt had been
made to solicit new members; and the work of the group had been
conducted privately, almost secretly. But this very secrecy, so far
from yielding seclusion, had been in part the cause of the suspicion
and notoriety which attached to its activities. Perhaps it was better
after all to come out into the open, to declare publicly its objectives,
and to canvass actively for a membership among the rank and file.
Such a policy was by no means inconsistent with Curtis's own view,
which was that there would come a time when the stage of inquiry
would give way to the stage of action. For, he had quoted, " 'lawyers
will have a hand in the matter, and politicians, and financiers and
poets and the clergy of all denominations; but although these lofty
personages will contribute their valuable ideas to the common stock
and will take a great deal of credit for the result, the man whose
judgment must be satisfied, in order that his steadfastness may
support the Union, is the man who sets off every morning with his
bag of tools and his breakfast wrapped in a handkerchief.' "[49]
The new policy brought new problems, of which one was the

[47]Dafoe Papers, G. M. Wrong to J. W. Dafoe, Sept. 20, 1916.
[48]Walker Papers, Sir Edmund Walker to H. G. Williams, Feb. 20, 1917.
[49]*Round Table Studies*, Series I, no. 1, 386.

organization of an expanded membership. In the summer of 1916 Lionel Curtis toured Canada in the company of G. M. Wrong to assess the prospects. They reported as follows:

In our opinion the movement ought to be centralised, and also decentralised. There should be a central office. . . . There should be a map showing where the Groups would work and a card register recording the Members of these Groups. On the other hand we recommend that the Dominion be mapped out in Provinces or Groups of Provinces and that one man should be made responsible for the organization of the work in each of these districts. . . . The Groups should be organized for the specific purpose of studying the Problem of the Commonwealth and the "Commonwealth of Nations" . . . and in this way a large number of people throughout Canada will become seized of the issues at stake before the time when Canada has to decide whether to demand to take part in an Imperial Convention such as that foreshadowed by Mr Asquith and Mr Lloyd George after peace is made. These Groups should include men of all parties. . . . The effect will be that whenever the issue is placed before the country, as it must be shortly after the War, the members of these Groups will know pretty clearly which side they are going to take. Militant organizations will then of necessity be formed. . . .

It is only by means such as these that the growth of the movement will be watched and its strength properly gauged. In short, the time is passed when the movement can be carried on by the present informal methods and in the spare time of a few busy men. If a vast amount of enthusiasm and interest already created in the Dominion is not to run to waste, it must be given a definite organization.[50]

Curtis added: "To cover Canada from Halifax to Victoria with these groups is the task of the next twelve months."[51]

This work was forthwith put in hand. Round Table groups sprang up from coast to coast. From Vancouver the regional Secretary reported that three groups were functioning in British Columbia and that a fourth, at Nanaimo, was in prospect.[52] In Manitoba, where the Dafoe influence was strong, there was distinctly less enthusiasm. "I have just returned from Winnipeg," a member of the newly created Round Table Council for Canada reported, "where I discussed Round Table matters. . . . There is no doubt whatever that The Round Table has received 'a black eye' in Winnipeg and it is useless to press just now for the creation of study groups in this district."[53]

[50]Walker Papers, copy of "Report of Professor Wrong and Mr Curtis on their Western Trip," July, 1916.

[51]Ibid., copy of Lionel Curtis to A. J. Glazebrook, July 5, 1916.

[52]Ibid., copy of G. F. Scott to A. J. Glazebrook, Sept. 24, 1916.

[53]Ibid., G. L. Beer to Sir Edmund Walker, June 2, 1917. A few days earlier Walker had written: "Visit from Vincent Massey about Round Table and Winnipeg. They are clearly interested much more in purely Canadian questions than in the Round Table." Ibid., Journal, II, 216, entry of May 21, 1917.

The expanded membership envisaged for this new phase of the movement's activities required a somewhat different method of approach than that to which it had been accustomed in the past.

The groups as they were originally constituted [wrote A. J. Glazebrook to Lord Milner] amounting at their greatest number to some three hundred members, were made up of a rather selected body of men to whom a more or less high level of study appealed; but directly you pass from members like these to a body of say three or four, or even five thousand men, you have to deal with a progressively less educated set of people. To deal with these will require an attenuation of intellectual quality and an increase of what we call punch. . . . The men who have to organize these groups and stimulate people to get together to study on the new level must necessarily be of a somewhat different quality. What they will need is simplicity and a sympathetic understanding with the man in the street. The gospel of study of the Round Table has now got to be interpreted in such a way that it will take hold of any man.[54]

An example of the application of this common touch is to be found in a letter to Glazebrook from a correspondent who had just joined the Orange Lodge: "When I get to know my way about, I propose to talk Round Table. They are a good lot of fellows, loyal to the last drop of blood. . . . I have a lantern slide lecture on the Royal Navy, and have contracted to give that to my Lodge; they will like the pretty pictures, and then I will move on to the organization of the Empire."[55]

The swift expansion of the Round Table movement provoked a good deal of interest and curiosity throughout the country. To avoid any repetition of past misunderstanding, the Round Table Council decided to hold a public meeting under its auspices—a new departure. The purpose of the meeting would be to explain the nature of the movement and to further its cause. It was held in Convocation Hall at the University of Toronto on April 27, 1917. "I presided," wrote Sir Edmund Walker, "opening with an explanation of the work of the Round Table. Meeting largely attended and in every way a success."[56] It was prominently reported in *The Times* —Sir John Willison saw to that—and its editor, in a letter to his Canadian correspondent, described it as "really the first overt sign of [The Round Table's] progress in the Dominions."[57]

Drafting a programme of action for this second stage of the movement presented some difficulty. What was needed was a compromise between the rigid formulas of Lionel Curtis, unacceptable to Cana-

---

[54]*Ibid.*, copy of A. J. Glazebrook to Lord Milner, March 8, 1917.
[55]*Ibid.*, copy of C. F. Hamilton to A. J. Glazebrook, May 27, 1917.
[56]*Ibid.*, Journal, II, 209–10, entry of April 27, 1917.
[57]*Ibid.*, Quoted in Sir John Willison to Sir Edmund Walker, May 16. 1917.

dian opinion, and some vague and shadowy agenda which, if adopted, might rob the movement of its vitality and distinctive character. A good deal of time was consumed during the spring and summer of 1916 drafting a manifesto which, it was hoped, would successfully launch the movement upon the stage of action. The group finally settled upon the following principles of agreement:

I. That Canada has shown her determination to preserve and strengthen the ties which now bind her to Great Britain and the other portions of the British Commonwealth.

II. That effective organization of the Empire does not involve any sacrifice of responsible government in doméstic affairs or the surrender of control over fiscal policy by any portion of the Empire.

III. That it is an inevitable development of responsible Government in the Dominions that they should assume their proportionate share in the defence of the Empire, and should have a voice in determining its relations with other states.

IV. That as soon as circumstances permit, political leaders throughout the Empire, irrespective of party, should meet to consider the problem.[58]

The manifesto was circulated for signature, Ontario Liberals being the first approached. An earnest attempt was made to push the document among French-speaking Canadians, but their reaction, while probably anticipated, was not what was hoped for. "Our harmless Memorandum," wrote Walker, "is referred to in the French press of Quebec as 'a dangerous Imperial manifesto.' "[59] Elsewhere, however, the response was not unimpressive. By the end of May, 1917, over a thousand signatures had been secured, and many of them were those of Liberals. But, as Walker noted, "while many Liberals . . . are with us, the Globe will oppose us, and doubtless force the party to do so."[60]

[58]*The Round Table in Canada: How the Movement Began: What it Hopes to Accomplish* (Toronto, Feb., 1917), 3–4. The text published in this pamphlet and as given to the press was considerably shorter than an earlier draft which, itself the result of much revision, contained an introductory paragraph dissociating the views of *The Problem of the Commonwealth* from those of the Round Table movement as such.

At the same time the London group was attempting to define the common ground on which its members might stand. Its programme, however, was too close to the Curtis position for the liking of the Canadian group, one of whose members, after reading the letter in which Philip Kerr set out the London view, wrote: "Would it be possible to get an agreement with respect to any of these debateable matters so as to base a constitution for the 'Round Table' . . . upon it, without compelling so many to withdraw that the movement would lose its influence & become discredited?" Walker Papers, unidentified and undated memorandum. See also *ibid.*, copy of Philip Kerr to A. J. Glazebrook, Nov. 22, 1916.

[59]*Ibid.*, Sir Edmund Walker to H. Bell-Irving, April 26, 1917.

[60]*Ibid.*, Journal, II, 209–10, entry of April 27, 1917.

Copies of the Manifesto were sent to the Prime Minister and the Leader of the Opposition. Laurier's inhospitable reaction has already been noted. Borden was more cordial. He had received a copy before Laurier had. It was sent on to him at London, where he was attending the Imperial War Conference, by Willison, as the result of an arrangement with the Toronto group,[61] and it reached him after he had sponsored what subsequently became famous as "Resolution IX." Borden replied:

Your letter . . . inviting me to express sympathy with the proposals embodied in "The Round Table" petition is before me. Shortly after reaching Great Britain I called into formal conference Mr Massey, General Smuts and Sir Joseph Ward. After several meetings the form of resolution as finally proposed by me was adopted. I moved it in the Conference, and it was carried unanimously. The British Government, to whom I had previously submitted the resolution, heartily concurred in its details. It embodies everything in the petition except the fourth paragraph.
    . . . it will be a very simple matter to comply with the request which you place before me. . . .[62]

The attitude of the Canadian Round Table movement towards the

[61]"As arranged last night had a long talk with Willison. He will send our memorandum to Sir Robert Borden without waiting for the later signatures, about 1000 in all. When it is completed it will go to Sir Robert and Sir Wilfrid officially. . . . I also urged Willison to write Sir Robert as to the general situation. . . . He can do anything with the country if he will only lead boldly." *Ibid.*, 214, entry of May 16, 1917.

[62]*Ibid.*, copy of Sir Robert Borden to Sir John Willison, n.d. The following letter from Walter Long, then Colonial Secretary in the United Kingdom Government, to Sir Robert Borden suggests that Borden may have put the Round Table case more explicitly in his informal conversations:
    "I have been thinking over the scheme you outlined to me & I hope you won't mind if I write you unofficially and as a friend.
    "The misfortune is that nearly all our 'would-be Alexander Hamiltons' know nothing of our people, nothing of the House of Commons, [and] I really believe do not care much for either.
    "Some questions occur to me. 1. Who is to preside over this Imperial assembly? 2. How are the members to be selected? 3. What is to follow from their deliberations? 4. If they are to have no power how long would they care to meet & do nothing but talk?
    "I have been in our House for 37 years, Lieut. Gov. & Gov. 31 years ago, & Cab. 22 years ago, & have been a close student of Parliament & of the people & I feel confident that this scheme would command no support worth having." (Borden Papers, 35379, Walter Long to Sir Robert Borden, Sept. 15, 1917.)
    On the other hand Borden does not appear to have been wholly convinced of the merits of the Round Table position. Before leaving for London, he discussed with J. W. Dafoe "the matter of Imperial reorganization with special reference to the Curtis scheme." Dafoe wrote: "I was very pleased to find that our views were in great measure in agreement. I should like to think that Canadians can rely upon him to stand up to his position under the pressures which will be put upon him when he reaches London." Dafoe Papers, J. W. Dafoe to Sir Clifford Sifton, Feb. 12, 1917.

constitutional innovations of 1917 was one of cautious expectation. "Meeting of Glazebrook, [Vincent] Massey, Willison and myself," wrote Sir Edmund Walker in his journal on January 25, 1918, "regarding Round Table matters. We decided that, the first step having been taken in forming an Imperial Cabinet, we should wait and see how this venture works before undertaking any further propaganda."[63] Its members, like many others, were unsure of the meaning of the protean Resolution IX and uncertain whether the so-called Imperial Cabinet was merely an improper analogy or the germ of a real executive of empire. One member of the Canadian Round Table Council expressed his anxiety lest "the insistence upon rigid institutions with clearly defined powers of coercion . . . were to disrupt the splendid solidarity that the Empire has exhibited throughout the war," and wondered whether the existing Imperial Conference and the new Imperial Cabinet might not "insensibly acquire the authority to act as the spiritual authority of the Commonwealth increased."[64] But another council member thought that "if after the war they do not do something to create a link for the Empire with authority to hold it together—we will be no better off, I think not so well off, to meet an Empire crisis than we are now."[65] With opinions thus divided, to wait and see was the only sensible course.

From London, meanwhile, came the suggestion that plans be made for "a convention of the representatives of all the Round Table groups as soon as possible after the war," to be held before the special Imperial Conference which the 1917 conference had urged should meet to settle the constitutional future of the Empire. The Round Table convention was to be "entirely open, in the sense that it should be free to come to any decision, e.g., to dissolve the movement altogether, to continue it as a purely student association, or to reconstitute it as a society of people holding definite views as to the solution of the Imperial problem."[66] This convention, like the proposed post-war Imperial constitutional conference, was never held. Perhaps the fact that the latter did not materialize caused the promoters of the Round Table convention to drop their plans. Or perhaps the same growing preoccupation with affairs at home, which lessened the interest of Dominion statesmen in implementing the suggestion of the Imperial Conference of 1917, caused the Round Table groups to change their minds.

[63]Vol. II, 287.
[64]Walker Papers, copy of G. F. Beer to A. J. Glazebrook, May 25, 1917.
[65]Ibid., Z. A. Lash to Sir Edmund Walker, Aug. 23, 1917.
[66]Ibid., copy of Acting Secretary, London Round Table, to Secretary of Toronto Round Table, Oct. 18, 1917.

Whatever the reason, the leading personalities of the Canadian Round Table movement no longer gave it priority in their scale of interests. Willison became absorbed in the Canadian Reconstruction Association; Walker devoted himself to assembling the Canadian War Records, to the National Gallery, and to travel. Wrong's correspondence betrays a continuing interest in the Imperial War Cabinet, but more obviously an assertion of nationalist feeling which drove all thoughts of imperial federation from his mind. Popular interest in the movement faded as quickly as it had appeared. The Canadian solution to the "problem of the Commonwealth" was left to develop along just those lines which Lionel Curtis had prophesied would lead to separation. The prophet is said to have been wrong. But it may still be too soon to tell.